Church and Disability

Reimagining Church as Event: Perspectives from the Margins
Series Editors: George Zachariah and Sudipta Singh

In these eleven volumes, a collective of Indian theologians envisions Church as an Event that happens in particular contexts in the life of the communities at the margins. They argue that in the life of the communities who experience on their bodies the violence and hegemony of dominant power relations, morality, and religious dogmas and practices, the church happens as countercultural experiences that disrupt the logic of the prevailing order. These experiences enable and empower them to affirm and celebrate their differences, knowledges and beauty even as they weave their liberation. Church as event is a call to rising to life, creating life-flourishing communities that live out the foretaste of the reign of God.

Titles in this Series

Church and Religious Diversity Joshua Samuel and Samuel Mall
Church and Gender Justice Aruna Gnanadason
Faith in the Age of Empire Y.T. Vinayaraj
Dalitekklesia: A Church from Below Raj Bharat Patta
Church and Climate Justice Vinod Wesley
Church and Disability Samuel George
Church and Diakonia in the Age of COVID-19 Mothy Varkey
Decolonising Oikoumene Gladson Jathanna
Church and Human Sexuality Arvind Theodore
With Many Voices: Liturgies in Context Viji Varghese Eapen (Ed.)
The Word becoming Flesh George Zachariah

Church and Disability

Samuel George

2020

Church and Disability- jointly published by the Indian Society for Promoting Christian Knowledge (ISPCK), Post Box 1585, Kashmere Gate, Delhi-110006 and Council for World Mission, Singapore-338729.

Online order: http://ispck.org.in/book.php

Also available on amazon.in

ISBN: 978-93-88945-84-4

Kindle Edition: 978-93-88945-97-4

Cover Illustration Credit : Immanuel Paul Vivekanandh K

Laser typeset by

ISPCK, Post Box 1585, 1654, Madarsa Road, Kashmere Gate, Delhi-110006 • *Tel:* 23866323

e-mail: ashish@ispck.org.in • ella@ispck.org.in
website: www.ispck.org.in

Dedicated to
The Ecumenical Disability Advocates Network-
World Council of Churches
(EDAN-WCC)
for its pioneering efforts in bringing disability
studies to the mainstream.

Contents

Foreword

Discernment and radical engagement (Dare) is an initiative of the Council for World Mission (CWM) to enable faith communities to *clarify what it means to engage in* public witness to God's justice and peace in a corrupt and conflicted world.

> The mission of Dare is conceived as the coming together of (a) the *radical soul* of discernment and sense-making in theology and biblical criticism; (b) the yearnings for *signifying engagement* that rise out of the slums of modernism and the valleys of despair; and (c) the commitment to redemption songs that *inspire disturbance* at the hubs of power.

As part of the DARE initiative, each region of CWM is invited to prepare and share biblical and theological resources on current themes and issues being considered by CWM, drawing upon the experiences and resources from the region.

Interfaith Engagement, Ecumenism and Inclusive communities against dehumanising social categorisations are the themes for the book series undertaken by the South Asia region of CWM. The thrust is centred on **Reimagining Church as Event: Perspectives from the Margins**. It calls to the fore persons living in the margins and highlights their voice, their narratives and their passion for a rearrangement of life in communities, as we know it, and a commitment to rise to life and to break out from Babylon. These books are intended for the use of lay people, pastors and evangelists as well as for theological students and seminaries. The series offer stories and narratives, analyses, liturgical resources, biblical, theological and ethical reflections, and missional/praxis proposals.

Church is an event that happens at the margins of contemporary life. Church happens as an epiphanic event where the divine presence is manifested and experienced in the pathos, struggles, contestations and harmonies of everyday existence. Church happens in those spaces where we celebrate the presence of Jesus, the Christ, in the flourishing of life. Church happens when we are transformed by one another, and inspired and enabled to engage in the transformative politics of the reign of God. Church happens whenever and wherever spirit-filled communities reclaim their subversive moral agency and contest the logic and practices of domination and exclusion. Church happens when the community experiences the healing power of the wounded healer and join Jesus in this risk-taking mission, despite the wounds we bear. To reimagine Church requires courage and commitment to engage in the mission of nurturing and organising communities of resistance and healing. This book series is a humble attempt at exposing and encouraging this radical expression of Church.

I appreciate and thank all those who are associated with this series, the authors, the contributors, the publishers and the editors. I commend this book series in the hope and prayers that they will help the faith communities in South Asia, and beyond, to *discern God's presence in community and dare to engage* in ways that re-present the God of life in communities and in the public square, *Rising to Life: Living out the New Heaven and New Earth.*

Colin Cowan
General Secretary
Council for World Mission

Introduction

*Wati Longchar**

Millions of people are pushed to the margins owing to injustice. Ableism, ageism, patriarchy, racism, tribalism, casteism and materialism are unjust structures that disenfranchise and dehumanise persons with disabilities. They are scorned, considered incapable and their failures are seen as a result of them being sinners, lazy and intellectually incapable. Persons with disabilities suffer most in the church and society from ableism.

Theological reflection from the perspective of persons with disabilities is almost silent in our theological discourses. Persons with disabilities, whose voices were never heard in the church and whose experiences were never considered in doing theology, are raising new theological questions: Are we not created in the 'image of God'? Is our disability a curse from God? Is our physical impairment the result of our parents' sin or our personal sin? Are we sinners? Why are we excluded from the church, which is for all? Why are we not given responsible positions in society? Why do people look upon us as inferior? How do we contribute our gifts to the life of the church and to society when we are not given any space? All these questions are crucial and Christian theology and the ministry of our church will remain incomplete without addressing these issues and concerns. Our society is incomplete without the recognition of the gifts of persons with disabilities. It demands a new way of reading the Bible, doing theology and ministerial practice. This research work attempts to address some of these theological questions.

Jesus stood for an inclusive community. He brought people with disability, the poor and the ones rejected by society to the centre of God's kingdom. Jesus challenged discriminatory practices and the callous attitudes of abled rich people. For instance, Jesus' act of healing a man with a shrivelled hand on the Sabbath (Mark 3:1-12) was a challenge to Jewish leaders. They did not want the man to be healed in the synagogue because for them the observance of Sabbath was more important than saving a life. They were afraid that this man would enter the synagogue with the ailment, which would defile the holy place. Religious rituals and laws were more important than saving a life. But for Jesus, life was more important. Jesus ignored religious rituals. Against their ritualism, Jesus said, "The Sabbath was made for humankind and not humankind for the Sabbath." Jesus healed that disabled person in spite of religious restrictions and the fact that the Pharisees were watching him. In Jesus' view, care and healing were of prime importance. Jesus stood for the cause of the sick and the disabled. He defended them against the prevailing attitude that suffering and physical impairment were due to sin. Jesus reached out to the sick and the disabled and touched them to bring healing. Jesus not only healed them of their physical infirmities, but also restored them to their rightful place in society. Because of his compassionate love for the disabled and the sick, Jesus did not hesitate to break the Sabbath law (Mk 3:1-6). Jesus' motive behind his healing ministry was not to present himself as a healer or magician but to start a movement of hope for the hopeless, a movement to bring someone from being a nobody to being somebody. On encountering Jesus, the sick and the disabled experienced the worth and dignity of life. In the kingdom of God, there is no sinner who cannot be made clean again.

We can imagine what Jesus would do for persons with disability today in our church and society. Jesus would not take the road of denial, discrimination, ostracisation and isolation. He would be there with them to bring healing, hope and restoration to the community, just as he did on many occasions. Jesus would certainly condemn the Pharisaic attitude of abled people. Therefore, it is our duty not to pass judgment and undermine them but to accept those with disability the way they are and minister to them with compassion, open-hearted acceptance, love and care. We should allow them to grow and contribute their gifts to the church and society. The continuing stigmatisation of people with disability calls on the church to ask what it means to be an inclusive community that Jesus envisioned and proclaimed. As a community of disciples of Jesus Christ, the church should be a sanctuary, a safe place, a refuge, a shelter for the stigmatised and the excluded. The disciples of Jesus are thus called to work for a church of all and for all.

The Council for World Mission (CWM), the Ecumenical Disability Advocates Network (EDAN) and the Programme for Theology and Cultures in Asia (PTCA) have drawn our attention to the fact that without the inclusion of persons with disabilities, we cannot talk about the unity of the church. There is no unity of churches without acknowledging the gifts of persons with disability. All people, with or without disabilities, are created in the image of God and are called to an inclusive community in which they are empowered to use their gifts. In fact, the world will be poorer without the contribution of persons with disabilities. Jesus loved and cared for them.

We need to affirm that diversity is an integral part of God's creation. Society—from its most basic unit, the family, to its broader forms, the church and the community—has to be a place where everyone, regardless of gifts and abilities, is genuinely welcome, given every opportunity to participate meaningfully and nurtured towards fulfilment. We need to work together more rigorously so that our common vision for the establishment of an inclusive, affirming and empowering global society may be realised. Let us strive to create a society and church where everyone, regardless of gifts and abilities, is genuinely included or else our churches will remain disabled communities without the inclusion of persons with disabilities.

For many years, disability was seen as a medical issue. Churches also pursued a charitable approach, assuming that disabled people are incapable. Today we need to address the disability issue as structural injustice. A community-oriented transformative *diakonia* is required. The church's ministry for disabled people needs to address the social dimension of inclusivity and the attitudinal change of abled people towards persons with disabilities. To remove the barriers to that, we need to equip theological educators, pastors and theological education for an inclusive society. Let us stand together towards helping society end discrimination, isolation and denial of opportunities for persons with disabilities. Let us affirm that persons with disabilities are not just a gift for the family and society, but also an opportunity for us to grow in love, mutual aid and unity as we are all called to be a gift to the other, to be Christ to our neighbours and to see Christ in our neighbours.

This volume adequately addresses the issues that are raised here and I commend the work of Dr. Samuel George for a wider readership both at lay and theological levels.

***The Rev. Dr. Wati Longchar** currently serves as Consultant for Theological Education in East Asia for the America Baptist Churches, USA. He served as the Dean of the Senate Centre for Extension and Pastoral Theological Research of the Senate of Serampore College (University), and as Professor of Theology & Cultures at the Yushan Theological College & Seminary, Taiwan.

Acknowledgements

"You cannot build a house on your own. You need others," said someone. It is so true of such a writing project. This work would not have been possible without the help of so many people.

It is to the late Dr. Samson Prabhakar (former director of SATHRI) that I owe my gratitude for introducing me to Disability Studies in 2006. Until then, I had never heard of such a field of study.

Since 2006, the Ecumenical Disability Advocacy Network (EDAN-WCC) has become my second "family." I am grateful to Dr. Samuel Kabue and Ms. Anjeline Okola for making me an important part of this movement. It is to them that I owe the most for making Disability Studies a part of my theological journey. This book is humbly dedicated to the pioneering and prophetic works of EDAN.

A word of appreciation for Dr. Wati Longchar, who was instrumental in bringing EDAN to India, and the various opportunities he provided me to engage with disability issues.

A very special thanks to the Council for World Mission (CWM) for the various opportunities (Zambia, India, Malaysia,

New Zealand) to engage on the issues of disability and church. And also, for publishing this work.

A special thanks to Dr. George Zachariah (Trinity Theological College, New Zealand) for initiating this work. His guidance and editorial expertise made this work publishable.

Some of the works that are included here were earlier published in various international journals and books, including *International Review of Mission*; *Ecumenical Review*; *Bangalore Theological Forum*; *Persons with Disabilities in Society: Problems and Challenges*; *Sprouts of Disability Theology*; *Disability Theology from Asia: A Resource Book for Theological and Religious Studies*. These are either reworked or enlarged according to the need of the volume.

Fourteen years of engagement with disability issues would not have been possible without the constant help and prayers of my family members, especially my wife Dr. Atula Ao.

Thank you, CWM, and ISPCK for making this book available to a wider audience.

Above all, I thank God for being the constant guide in my journey of faith and theology.

Deo Gloria!

Chapter 1

Disability Ministry:
A Call to the Church

Introduction

Can the church think of such a ministry? Before we venture into the WHY and HOW of the church's Disability Ministry, it is better to clarify certain terminologies used. We do this in the context of the Global South(s), specifically the Indian subcontinent.

Disability

Disability is all that imposes restrictions on disabled people and, as such, disablement is nothing to do with the body.[1] Therefore, disability, like racism or sexism, is discrimination and social oppression. Disabled people are those people with impairments who are disabled by society.[2] In that sense, disability is a condition that is imposed from outside.

Ministry

In Christian theology, the word ministry has a two-pronged meaning—a *general* and a *particular* meaning. In its general sense, it means all Christians are called to ministry and are empowered for this task by the Holy Spirit. It is what we often allude to as the Reformation tradition—"priesthood of all believers." In its particular meaning, it means an office that is ordained by God to provide for regular and responsible preaching of the gospel, celebration of the sacraments and leadership in the life and service of the church.[3]

An interesting understanding of the biblical notion of ministry is that this gospel is conveyed as "treasures in clay jars" (2 Cor. 4:7). Ministry is carried out by fallible human beings. It is in and through our human frailty, human weakness and human inadequacies that we find God's promise and grace manifested in our lives. God is not embarrassed by our humanity. God uses us to be a channel of blessing and transformation of others.

Ministry is inclusive. God summons everyone to the ministry irrespective of colour, creed, gender, race, sexual orientation and ability. No one should be excluded. If so, why are Persons with Disabilities (PWDs) being excluded from the ministry of the church?

Disability in the Global South(s)

The phrase "Global South" refers broadly to the regions of Latin America, Asia, Africa and Oceania. It is one of a family of terms, including "Third World" and "Periphery," that denote regions outside Europe and North America, mostly (though not all) low-income and often politically or culturally marginalised. The use of the phrase Global South marks a shift from a central focus on development or cultural difference towards an emphasis on geopolitical relations of power.[4]

In a broader sense, it references an entire history of colonialism, neo-imperialism and differential economic and social change through which large inequalities in living standards, life expectancy and access to resources are maintained.[5]

Disability studies (or perspective) in the Global South(s) is something "new" and not taken so seriously. However, as a formal area of academic inquiry, it has been making significant strides in the Global North since the 1990s with rigorous interdisciplinary scholarship and the emergence of several full-fledged academic programmes.[6] Whereas, in India and other countries of the Global South(s) it is in a relatively nascent stage.

Anita Ghai rightly points out:

> When you think of a new academic programme, the usual pattern is to find a list of scholars who 'do' whatever they are looking for—sociology, history, psychology, education and so on. It is, however, extremely rare to find someone who 'does' Disability Studies (DS) because of the historical myopia towards disability within academia. As is the case with women and gender studies, a disability perspective has been considered to be too limiting to be of any epistemological significance.[7]

Disability was not even studied, let alone it being a perspective/methodology in academia. At the most, it was considered for charitable or some social services. Ghai further writes, "So much of disability history has entailed the grouping together of disabled people through techniques of surveillance, identification and nomenclature."[8]

Roughly, more than 15 per cent of the world's population is affected by disability, including physical and sensory impairments, developmental and intellectual disability, and psychosocial disability.[9] Going by that percentage, India has the largest concentration of PWDs in the world.

Historically it is noted that among the various social services in the Global South(s), disability issues are at the bottom. There are other "priorities" to be met in such countries. It is because of these reasons that issues of PWDs in Global South(s) do not find much mention. It is in this context that we need to understand the plight of PWDs. Some of these are discussed in detail in other articles found in this volume.

Disability perspective is both unique and important. It enlightens how individuals designated 'disabled' are treated in a manner that diminishes their economic, interpersonal, psychological, cultural, political and physical well-being, relegating them to membership in a minority group. Disability perspective can enable academia and society to think critically about not only disability but also about oppressions that affect all historically marginalised groups.[10]

Nilika Mehrotra claims that disability studies originated from activism across various Western contexts, including India.[11] This has created its own share of opportunities and limitations for disability studies.

Ghai writes,

> On the one hand, disability studies is grounded in lived realities of disability and emphasises emancipatory research. But, on the other hand, disability studies risks inheriting some of the limitations of disability studies activism, including a limited focus on intersectionality, a problematisation of the public/ private divide, limited focus on the heterogeneity of disability and so on.[12]

Disability studies in the Global South(s) has not been privileged within academia, perhaps because the understanding of disability is intimately connected to the study of ignorance, invisibility and identity as academia has not evolved tools for understanding how and why various forms of knowing have 'not come to be,' or disappeared, or have been delayed or long neglected, for better or for worse, at various points in history. The absence of disability from the mainstream academia creates and maintains a status quo where the 'disabled' are incorporated within the existing social patterns as 'problems'.[13] Disability in Global South(s) remains neglected both politically and academically. However, a serious academic approach to disability studies is very crucial for it to become mainstream in our cultural, political and even religious conversations. Why disability studies?

Ghai writes,

> An academic understanding of disability as a social, cultural and political phenomenon, I believe, externalizes the issue and helps counter the notion of disability as an inherent, unchallengeable trait located in an individual. Such an approach rejects the view that disability is solely a medical problem or a personal tragedy. Disability studies, thus, places the responsibility for re-examining and repositioning the place of disability within society and academics and not on the individual. Disability studies may be many things to many people, but if its full potential is to be realised, then it must avoid being seen as simply a new bottle for old wine.[14]

A critical approach to disability studies can enable academia to think critically not only about disability, but also about oppressions that affect all historically marginalised groups.[15]

However, in our discussion we should not neglect the other areas of human conversation. Though a significant connection between academics and activism is critical, the metaphysical aspects of disability deserve equal merit.[16] It is this holistic approach to disability that we address in this volume on church and disability. That will include religion, spirituality, the Bible, ministry, mission, theology and theological education.

Why Disability Ministry?

As noted above, over 15 per cent of the world's population are PWDs. If so, how can the church neglect this important constituent of its life and ministry? It is only through a dedicated ministry of disability that both PWDs and others can be ministered.

Jesus said, "I will build my church." Theology has discussed *Ekklesia* for centuries. Is it the building or an institution or the people that Jesus refers to as "church"? Also, of interest is the ongoing (or even futuristic) nature of that call. What kind of church did Jesus envisage? A church of the elites, the able-bodied? What/who constitutes the church that Jesus spoke about?

Historically, it is noted that the church as an institution has not been very "kind" to PWDs. Nancy L. Eiesland rightly points out the condition (or relation) of the church with PWDs:

> The history of the church's interaction with the disabled is at best an ambiguous one. Rather than being a structure for empowerment, the church has more often supported societal structures and attitudes that have treated people with disabilities as objects of pity and paternalism. For many disabled persons, the church has been a "city on a hill"—physically inaccessible and socially inhospitable.[17]

For the church to become a body of justice for PWDs and other marginalised groups, it has to undergo radical liberative changes. It is hoped that this volume will at least "tickle" the soul of the church in this direction.

How Disability Ministry?

Can (should) we have specialised ministries for PWDs? Are these only for "them"? Some of these questions will come for further discussion in this volume. If the ministries of the church have to become holistic, then paradigmatic changes have to happen in its life, ministry and mission. What can PWDs contribute to this? How can they do it? This volume will help us in understanding some of these questions that are raised here.

Endnotes

[1] M. Oliver, *Understanding Disability: From Theory to Practice* (Basingstoke: Palgrave, 1996), 35.

[2] Quoted in Jenny Morris, "Impairment and Disability: Constructing an Ethics of Care That Promotes Human Rights," *Hypatia* 16, no. 4 (2001): 2.

[3] Daniel L. Migliore, *Faith Seeking Understanding: An Introduction to Christian Theology*, 2nd ed. (Michigan, Grand Rapids: William B. Eerdmans Publishing Company, 2004 (1993)), 296.

[4] Nour Dados, and Raewyn Connell, "The Global South," *Context* 11, no. 1 (Winter 2012): 12.

[5] Ibid., 13.

[6] Anita Ghai, "Introduction: Epistemological and Academic Concerns of Disability in the Global South," in *Disability in South Asia: Knowledge and Experience*, ed. Anita Ghai (New Delhi: Sage Publications, 2018), 23-24.

[7] Ibid., 24-25.

[8] Ibid., 25.

[9] WHO's report on disability (2011).

[10] Ghai, "Introduction: Epistemological and Academic Concerns of Disability in the Global South," 26.

[11] Nilika Mehrotra, "Disability Rights Movement in India: Politics and Practice," *Economic & Political Weekly* 46, no. 6 (2011): 65–72.

[12] Ghai, "Introduction: Epistemological and Academic Concerns of Disability in the Global South," 29-30.

[13] Ibid., 31.

[14] Ibid., 32.

[15] Ibid., 33.

[16] Ibid., 39.

[17] Nancy L. Eiesland, *The Disabled God. Towards a Liberatory Theology of Disability* (Nashville: Abingdon Press, 1994), 20.

Chapter 2

Doing Theology from an Indian Christian Disability Perspective

A Personal Note

I start my deliberations on a personal note because every theology is a personal faith reflection. I was born 'normal.' At the age of two months I was afflicted with polio, which almost crippled my legs. In the early 1970s (in India) the polio vaccine was administered three months after the birth of the child, and I was afflicted before that period. My parents were devastated. They did everything to get its impact reversed or at least minimise the effect of polio. I started 'walking' at the age of four. My parents took me to various medical facilities and I was given the unbearable callipers to walk with, which I hated so much not because it was cumbersome but it was painful too. Due to the non-disabled friendly infrastructural facilities almost everywhere, I had to undergo much physical and emotional trauma. At the ages of 14 and 16 I underwent two corrective operations which, to a great extent, made me independent. Right now, I do almost everything that a 'normal' person does. I ride a bicycle and a bike, drive cars, about which I often hear critical comments.

But there is another side to this story. My parents were missionaries in the northernmost part of India, Jammu and Kashmir. They took me to various 'healing' crusades for the reversal of the effects of polio (I don't belittle them, because they wanted me to be 'normal' like any other kid). I remember people praying for my 'healing' and telling me to be strong in my faith because it is faith that heals. (So, is there no healing if there is no faith?) People would sympathise with me and said that they prayed for me. Gradually, I saw a shift in people's perspective and attitude. They no longer sympathised with me but advised me that one had to accept and live faithfully with whatever "thorn" God had given us.

The most painful experience that I have undergone, for almost eight years now, is in choosing a life partner. I come from a context where marriages are mostly arranged by parents. My parents have done everything they could (they still do and pray for a life partner for me), but all their efforts have been in vain so far. I am the most theologically qualified person in the state of Jammu and Kashmir. A person with my educational qualification will get any life partner of his/her choice, but I will not because I am not 'normal'. A friend left me as she was forced to do so by her parents because they thought I am disabled and now she lives happily with an 'able-bodied' person. I often get offended by the questions they raise. It is interesting that many who ask such questions (sometime nasty too) have severe illnesses which could even kill them soon, but they think I have an illness and not them.

It is in this context of constant pain (mostly emotional) and struggle that my theological expressions are formulated.

The above biographical note touches on various aspects of disability such as religio-cultural, socio-political, emotional, spiritual and theological. This paper touches on some of these issues from an Indian perspective.

Disability Defined

The field of disability studies is a new arrival in academic humanities.[1] It focuses on the disabled body in its manifold locations in time and space: the history of disability, the metaphysics or theologies that attempt to place deviant bodies in a cosmic order, the social construction of disability by the able-bodied and the lived experience of people with disabilities. Since disability studies emerged from comparative literature and contemporary sociology, the focus of major works in the field has been on the modern era. The medical model of disability, which dominated the nineteenth and early twentieth centuries, thought about disability, viewed it simply as a biological condition to be cured, if possible. Confinement to the home and institutionalisation resulted from this emphasis. In recent decades, activists and scholars have instead proposed a social-functional model of disability. This approach draws a distinction between biological conditions and a lack of fit between a given body type and built social structures. Thus, a sensory deficit is called *impairment*. The term *disability* refers to functional limitations that result from the combination of impairment and the social environment.[2]

Defining disability is difficult to accommodate the expectation of all disability groups. Disability signifies what a person suffering impairment cannot be and cannot do. The following definitions of disability will help us understand it more wholly.

- E. Helander gave the simplest and may be the initial definition of a disabled person: "A person who in his/her society is regarded as disabled, because of a difference in appearances and/or behaviour:" In most instances, a disabled person has functional limitations and/or activity restrictions. A 'functional limitation' disability may be defined as "specific reductions in bodily functions that are described at the level of the person." 'Activity restriction' disability may be defined as "specific reductions in daily activities that are described at the level of the person."[3]

- Disability is a relative term because cultures define differently their norms of being and doing. Disability may be identified by appearance—"ugliness," albinism, the absence of a digit (even a functionally unimportant one)—while impairments (mild to moderate mental retardation, club foot) recognised as disabling in Western cultures are often not treated as disabling.[4]

According to the Persons with Disabilities (Equal Opportunities, Protection of Rights and Full Participation) Act, 1995, a disabled person is one who suffers not less than 40 per cent of any disability as certified by a medical authority. The disabilities identified are blindness, low vision, cerebral palsy, leprosy, leprosy cured, hearing impairment, locomotor disability, mental illness and mental retardation, as well as multiple disabilities.

- According to the National Sample Survey Organisation (NSSO), India, which conducted surveys of persons with disabilities in 1981, 1991 and 2002 in India, disability is, "Any restriction or lack of abilities to perform an activity in the manner or within the range considered

> normal for human being." It excludes illness /injury of recent origin (morbidity) resulting into temporary loss of ability to see, hears, speak or move.

The term "disability" is a creation of modern society in its attempt to group people with different characteristics perceived to have related or similar effects on human life. The dictionary meaning of disability is "the condition of being unable to perform as a consequence of physical or mental unfitness." Surprisingly, the Judaeo-Christian tradition did not have this type of classification as it described individuals as suffering from specific infirmities. This explains the reason for this term's non-inclusion in the Bible. There are various other terms used to call people with disability: impaired, handicapped, differently abled. These definitions often fall under two main classifications, namely, the medical model and the social model. Caregivers, health workers and academics have largely embraced the medical model, while persons with disabilities, through their movements, are largely proponents of the social model.

'Disabled' India

I may sound very agitated in using the term "disabled" India, but the following facts and figures will help us understand the reason for my using this term.

India is the second most populated country in the world with over one billion people. It is a land of varied facets. It is estimated that over 30 million persons are with some kind of disability in the Indian Union.[5] The Indian subcontinent has the dubious distinction of having the largest geographical concentration of disabled persons on this planet.[6]

The reality that disability discourse was given negligible status in Indian society can be construed by the fact that the

1981 Census of India was the first and last twentieth century census to enumerate the disabled. In it they were classified as "blind", "dumb" and "crippled." Extreme criteria of impairment were used in it. As a result, only 1.1 million were identified as disabled.[7]

According to the Census 2001, there are 2.19 crore persons with disabilities in India who constitute 2.13 per cent of the total population. This includes persons with visual, hearing, speech, locomotor and mental disabilities. Seventy-five per cent of persons with disabilities live in rural areas, 49 per cent of the disabled population is literate and only 34 per cent are employed. It is also estimated that there are 93.01 lakh women with disabilities, which constitute 42.46 per cent of the total disabled population.[8] Women with disabilities are in a more precarious condition. They require protection against exploitation and abuse.

It should be noted that the above-mentioned figures may not represent the true picture of PWDs in India because statistics from the United Nations suggests that 7-10 per cent of the world's population have some form of physical or mental disability.[9]

If measured by resources committed and by available data, alleviating the condition of PWDs is the lowest priority on state welfare agendas in practically all underdeveloped countries and, arguably, in all countries. In India, positive discrimination for disabled people lags long behind that for the Scheduled Castes and the Scheduled Tribes.[10] On India's social welfare agenda, poverty, caste and gender push disability issues to the bottom. This low priority can be explained by the political weakness of disabled people due to high perceived economic costs and low perceived political benefits of a state response to problems that are administratively anomalous.

One can understand the condition of the disabled in India[11] by the sheer magnitude of the population living under the poverty line. In rural areas, the disabled mostly manage their livelihood by begging.[12] Things are not better in the urban set-up. PWDs are a great economic and mental drag to parents and guardians.[13] With the magnitude of the problems of our variously disabled added to the unemployment levels and underdevelopment among the 'normal', and our limited resources spread over numerous pressing demands, the funds that we can spare for the rehabilitation of the severely disabled are likely to remain relatively small for quite some time. The inevitable conclusion is that we will not be able to treat and rehabilitate even one-hundredth of the disabled population institutionally for the next decade or two.[14]

I have a twin-foci in this paper:

Social Responsibility

Physical disability is a deviation from the socially valued bodily characteristics of an individual in a given society.[15] The presence of such persons in society would definitely give rise to special problems that the community at large has to deal with. Failure to cope with those special issues and demands would affect the society as a whole.

The non-disabled majority tend to maintain a certain social distance, often treating the disabled as outsiders. Many 'normal' people feel uncomfortable in the presence of a disabled person. Some find it very difficult to accept and mingle with the disabled as they do with other people; and since they have greater prestige and power, this can restrict the opportunities of the handicapped. Often, they are forced either to associate with each other or become socially isolated. They are frequently segregated—physically, psychologically and socially. The disabled person, sensing social discrimination, gravitates to his/her own kind who can accept him/her without discrimination. It is in the economic sphere that discrimination against the physically handicapped is found to be more overt and serious.[16] Their economic security is often threatened by the frequent refusals of work opportunities in many areas of employment.

The social effects of physical disability tend to create social distance between the disabled and their families on the one side and the community on the other. This distance is often expressed by the non-acceptance of the handicapped in social functions, religious services, educational programmes, workplaces and marital relationships, leading to social and economic isolation.[17]

In India, the earlier emphasis on medical rehabilitation has now been replaced by an emphasis on social rehabilitation. There has been an increasing recognition of abilities of persons with disabilities and emphasis on mainstreaming them in society on the basis of their capabilities.

The disabled in India need both change in social attitudes and help. It is known that the social attitudes of the non-disabled affect the social integration of disabled people. "The more severe and visible the deformity is, the greater is the fear of contagion, hence the attitude of aversion and segregation towards the crippled."[18] Ignorance of needs and capabilities may hinder social relationships. Disabled people may be feared as evil, as cursed or spiritually afflicted.[19]

Attitudes reinforced by religious institutions may militate against rehabilitation or integration, although the great religious traditions may contain their own contradictions. Treatment and training may be understood as defiance to the will of Allah or as interference with a person's karma. While giving alms to beggars is pious behaviour, some Hindu religious organisations and temple trusts, many of them very wealthy, do not think it part of their duty to help the disabled as they consider a handicap to be the result of the victim's misdeeds in his/her previous life.[20]

This is the condition of the disabled in India, shunned by society and sanctioned by religion. The need of the hour is social integration of the disabled into the mainstream of society. They also need uncorrupt help to gain access to any benefits the state may feel obliged to provide them.

Some years back, the National Policy on Disability in India was formulated. The Constitution of India ensures equality, freedom, justice and dignity of all individuals and implicitly mandates an inclusive society for all, including persons with disabilities. In the recent years, there have been vast and positive changes in the perception of society towards persons with disabilities. It has been realised that a large number of persons with disabilities can have a better quality of life if they have equal opportunities and effective access to rehabilitation measures.

The National Policy recognises that PWDs are a valuable human resource for the country and seeks to create an environment that provides them equal opportunities, protects their rights and encourages full participation in society. The focus of the policy are:

- Prevention of Disabilities

- Rehabilitation Measures: It includes (i) physical rehabilitation, which includes early detection and intervention, counselling and medical interventions and provision of aids and appliances. It will also include the development of rehabilitation professionals;

(ii) Educational rehabilitation, including vocational education; and (iii) economic rehabilitation for a dignified life in society.

Acts Related to Disability in India

There are some legal provisions for the disabled in India. But these are often criticised as mere tokenistic. The reason being that in the formulation of the Acts, there was little input from the disabled themselves.[21]

- *The Persons with Disabilities (Equal Opportunities, Protection of Rights and Full Participation) Act, 1995*

The Act is guided by the philosophy of empowering persons with disabilities and their associates. Its endeavour has been to introduce an instrument for promoting equality and participation of persons with disability on the one hand, and eliminating discriminations of all kinds on the other.

- *The Rehabilitation Council of India Act, 1992*

The Act was created to provide for the constitution of the Rehabilitation Council of India for regulating training of the rehabilitation professional, the maintaining of a Central Rehabilitation Register and other matters relating to these issues.

- *The Mental Health Act, 1987*

An Act to consolidate and amend the law relating to the treatment and care of mentally ill persons, to make better provisions with respect to their affairs properly and for matters connected therewith or incidental thereto.

- *The National Trust for the Welfare of Persons with Mental Retardation and Cerebral Palsy Act, 1999*

The government has also introduced a National Trust for the Welfare of Persons with Mental Retardation and Cerebral Palsy Bill, 1995. The trust aims to provide total care to persons with mental retardation and cerebral palsy and also manage the properties bequeathed to the trust.

- *Employees' State Insurance Act, 1948*

This provides for facilities for persons employed in government agencies and public sector organisations to avail themselves of various benefits.

- *Exemptions on Income Tax Act*

There are special provisions in the Income Tax Act for persons with disability and for the parents/legal guardians of persons with disability. The relevant sections are reproduced below.

Section 80 U of the Income Tax Act, 1961: Allows an exemption of ₹40,000 from the income of the assessee with disability.

Section 80 DD of the Income Tax Act, 1961: Parent or relative upon whom the person with disability is dependent is allowed deductions of ₹40,000 for maintenance, which includes medical treatment of person with disability.

- *The All India Service (Special Disability Leave) Regulations, 1957*

With all these policies and laws there is no doubt there is a concerted effort to address the issue of disability in India both at the administrative and general levels. But one has to confess that the problem is so severe that there is much to be done. Only then can a sense of social security be created among PWDs.

Theological Responsibility

Christianity affirms that humanity is created in God's image. It is in that image we are united. But in that very unity lies diversity, reflected in the fact that we are created different as men and women. Difference is God-given. It is God's intention for humanity.[22] In this understanding, there is no "normal" way for humans to live. With this understanding, the notion of being "normal" could be viewed as oppressive. With this understanding, persons with disabilities may be understood as one minority group among many minority groups.[23]

This notion challenges the traditional theological interpretation of disability. Earlier, people with disability were seen as "weak vessels" that needed to be handled with care. They were objects of charity. More precisely, they were objects of the church's need to do good deeds.[24] The changed perceptions about PWDs has created a differing notion now. They are no longer objects of pity and charity but equal partners in the ministry and mission of God in the realisation of the kingdom of God. The language of the ecumenical movement becomes pertinent in these discussions. Is the one body of Christ whole without people with disabilities? If we profess one Lord, one faith, one baptism, one God and Father of all (Eph. 4:5-6), what does that say about the church's approach to people with disabilities?

With this shift through the new understanding of disability, a fresh look at the New Testament notion of weakness is needed. Arne Fritzson asks:

> What does it mean that God chose what is weak in the world to shame the strong (1 Cor. 1:27)? What of the words that "the parts of the body which seem to be weaker are indispensable?" (1 Cor. 12:22). Notice that St. Paul here writes "seem to be" and not "are." Consider the strange words that the Lord gave St Paul in 2 Cor. 12:29, "My grace is sufficient for you, for my power

is made perfect in weakness." Do they have any import when the churches reflect on their response to people living with disabilities? Can a church that is not open to the gifts from the parts of the body that seem weaker learn where the power of the Lord is made perfect? PWDs' point of great weakness can ultimately become their great strength. Such is the journey and mystery of the cross.[25]

With this new shift, a kind of equality has entered the discussion around the church's way of meeting people with disabilities. Churches in India have to take a pro-disability stand. She has to move from advocacy to more a pragmatic and practical stand. She has to create a barrier-free environment for the social, theological and spiritual integration of the disabled. Jesus' most disabling experience was the experience on the cross when he cried out, "Why have you forsaken me, oh God?" It is this experience of Jesus' disability that gives people with disability a sense of belongingness. Jesus became disabled and identified with the disabled of this world. The church that does not identify with the disabled does not profess the true Lord Jesus Christ who himself became disabled.

Endnotes

[1] Rebecca Raphael, "Things Too Wonderful: A Disabled Reading of Job," *Perspectives in Religious Studies* 31, no. 4 (Winter 2004): 399.

[2] Ibid., 400.

[3] Quoted in Bupinder Zutshi, *Disability Status in India- Case Study of Delhi Metropolitan Region* (New Delhi: PhD Centre for the Study of Regional Development, Jawaharlal Nehru University, September 2004).

[4] Susan Erb and Barbara Harriss-White, *Outcast From Social Welfare. Adult Disability, Incapacity and Development in Rural South India* (Bangalore: Books for Change, 2002), 4.

[5] Ibid., xi.

[6] Ibid., xii.

[7] Ibid., 3.

⁸ http://www.disabilityindia.org. Accessed on 01/04/2007.

⁹ Lynda Katsuno and Arne Fritzson, "Disability," in *Dictionary of the Ecumenical Movement*, ed. Nicholas Lossky et al. (Geneva: WCC Publications, 2002), 326.

¹⁰ Erb and Harriss-White, xiii.

¹¹ For a detailed view on PWDs in India refer to Zutshi.

¹² There are instances where the family members of the disabled force them to beg and earn their livelihood.

¹³ Jainendra Kuman Jha, ed., *Encyclopaedia of Social Work* (Lucknow: Institute for Sustainable Development, 2001), 208.

¹⁴ Ibid., 209.

¹⁵ Jose Murickan and Georgekutty Kareparampil, *Persons with Disabilities in Society* (Trivandrum, India: Kerala Federation of the Blind, 1995), 1.

¹⁶ Ibid., 18.

¹⁷ Ibid., 19.

¹⁸ Arvindrai N. Desai, *Helping the Handicapped: Problems and Prospects* (New Delhi: Ashish Publishing House, 1990), 19.

¹⁹ P. Coleridge, *Disability, Liberation and Development* (Oxford: Oxfam, 1993), 71. Quoted in Erb and Harriss-White, 9.

²⁰ Quoted in Erb and Harriss-White, 9.

²¹ Ibid., 20.

²² Arne Fritzson and Samuel Kabue, *Interpreting Disability*, Risk Book (Geneva: WCC Publications, 2004), 5.

²³ Ibid., 7.

²⁴ Ibid., 10.

²⁵ Katsuno and Fritzson, 326.

Chapter 3

Reimagining the Image of God: Perspectives from Disabled Bodies

Introduction

Theologising in the context of India demands a radical shift in its approach and perspective. Theology, in a sense, is a *verb*, not a *noun*. Therefore, theology is **doing** (preaching, reflecting, writing, defending—*apologia*, praying and singing). It is an ongoing process. To do theology is to contextualise one's faith.[1] And to contextualise one's faith, one needs the right, appropriate and relevant sources. However, traditional theological positionings in India are often colonial, confessional (and denominational), dogmatic, male-centred, elitist, devoid of subaltern voices (Dalit, Adivasi, Tribal, Women, Disabled) and ecologically insensitive.[2] In most cases, the voices of the margins have been neglected and rejected in theologising. In this essay, an argument is made for theologising from the perspectives of the margins—that of the disabled.

Defining Theology: An Attempt

Even though the word theology comes from the Greek words *theos* (God/Divine) and *logos* (word/discourse), over the years it has been understood in various ways. For some, it is a systematic analysis of the nature, purposes and activity of God. And for some others, it is also understood as "the discipline of sacred learning" (Peter Abelard and Gilbert de la Porree). John Macquarrie writes, "Theology may be defined as the study which, through participation in and reflection upon a religious faith, seeks to express the content of this faith in the clearest and most coherent language available."[3] It can also mean a systematic study of the fundamental ideas of the Christian faith. Karl Rahner writes, "Theology is the science of faith. It is the conscious and methodical explanation and explication of the divine revelation received and grasped in faith."[4]

Renowned Christian theologian Raimundo Panikkar calls it *Cosmotheandrism*.[5] Roger Haight describes it succinctly,

> Theology today may be understood as a discipline, which seeks to understand and determine the underlying truth of all reality. Christian theology does not merely talk about God. Rather theology attempts to construe all things, world, human existence, human history and society, as well as God from within the vision that is mediated to the Christian community by its religious symbols.[6]

Theology, therefore, is human *words/discourses* about the "God-Human-Creation" relationship. Theology is also a construction. It needs sources for its composition and development. It draws upon a number of sources. This essay is an attempt to delineate the various sources of theology and how margin as a tool challenges and reimagines theology today.

I start with a few clarifications on the topic 'Image of God.' Image of God can be seen from two perspectives. Human beings made in the image of God and human beings' understanding about the image of God. Are they related? Here is an effort to decipher the concept of the image of God from a disability perspective.

My theological foundations are very much entrenched in two foundational theological treatises namely, John Macquarrie's *Principles of Christian Theology*[7] and Daniel L. Migliore's *Faith Seeking Understanding*.[8] Over the years, these have been my learning and teaching partners. This paper too would borrow certain ideas from them as we engage with the concept of the image of God. First, we look at human beings made in the image of God and, thereafter, how human beings perceive the image of God. In conclusion, we propose the disabled image of God, which is a theology from the margins.

Human Beings as Image of God

Human beings are a mystery unto themselves. The following sayings will throw some light on the intriguing nature of humankind.

Shakespeare exclaims, "What a work of art?" D. H. Lawrence writes, "Men [sic]! The only animal in the world to fear." Rabindranath Tagore writes, "Men [sic] are cruel, but Man [sic] is kind." Mark Twain opines, "Man [sic]—a creature made at the end of the week's work when God was tired." Oscar Wilde writes, "I sometimes think that God in creating man [sic] somewhat overestimated His ability." Josh Billings says, "Man [sic] was created a little lower than the angels, and has been getting lower ever since." All the above statements point to the fact that human beings are perceived as a combination of both good and evil.

Interpretation of 'Image of God' in historical theology

Biblically the concept of the 'image of God' is found in Genesis 1:26-27: "Let us make humankind in our image, according to our likeness…. So, God created humankind in his image, in the image of God he created them; male and female he created them." Image of God has been interpreted differently in the history of Christian theology.

'Image of God' as *physical resemblance* to God

Many argue that human beings in their upright stature have a physical resemblance to God. There are biblical passages that picture God anthropomorphically (cf. Gen. 3:8ff.). However, the biblical warrant is to forbid any kind of image-making of God (cf. Exo. 20:4).

'Image of God' as the *capacity to reason*

Middle Age theological doctor Thomas Aquinas, along with many others, view human rationality as a participation in and reflection of the divine logos by which the world was created. The problem is, if the essence of being human is seen primarily in the process of abstract reasoning by which the physical dimension of life is transcended, a corresponding depreciation of the emotional and physical dimensions of human existence is the result.[9]

'Image of God' as the capacity to have *dominion over the earth*

Some people view the concept of human beings bearing the image of God as resembling God in exercise of power and dominion over other creatures. The problem with this interpretation is that it creates a hierarchical pattern: God rules over the world, the soul controls the body, men are masters over women and children, and humanity dominates other creatures. Such an interpretation of human beings as the image of God legitimises reckless exploitation of God's created order.

Dorothée Wilhelm suggests a feminist-liberation-theological retrieval of the Decalogue's prohibition of images as a possible way out of the hierarchical domination over others. She writes,

> 'Don't make any images' means, you should not try to get power over your co-creatures. They are all creatures of God. Do not make them into lifeless images which fit into your catalogue of undesirable traits. Do not destroy their possibilities of living differently. Respect all persons. Every one of them is holy in a special way.[10]

'Image of God' as *human freedom*

There are those who interpret human beings as free, self-determining and self-transcending. They are both self-creators and creators of a world of culture that they impose upon the order of nature. In this free creative activity, human beings reflect the free creativity of God and thus become the image of God in the world.[11] There is a serious flaw with this understanding. Such unfettered freedom has the tendency to become independent (to an extreme level) and it can lead to self-gratification.

'Image of God' as *human life in relationship* with God and other created order

The first creation story describes God creating humankind in God's image; God created them male and female. To be human is to live freely and gladly in relationships of mutual respect and love. This paradigmatic form reflects the life of God as the triune God who eternally lives not in solitary existence but in community.

Daniel Migliore writes, "The image of God is not like an image permanently stamped on a coin. It is more like an image reflected in a mirror."[12] Human beings are created for life in a relationship that mirrors or corresponds to God's own life in relationship—the *Trinitarian relationship*. As the incarnate Lord lived in solidarity with humanity, so also the eternal God lives in a triune society of love which is open to the world; so humanity in its coexistence with others is intended to be the creaturely reflection of the living God.

"Image of God" in Christian theology cannot be understood without a Christological paradigm because, for Christian faith, Jesus Christ is the fullest expression of what God intends humanity to be. He becomes the paradigm for defining human beings as the image of God.

This brings us to the major focus of the paper—how do we perceive human beings created in the image of God, especially PWDs? How are we to see them as "equally" created in the image of God? Certainly, we cannot follow the paradigms of *physical resemblance, capacity to reason, dominion over others* and *pure human freedom*. That leaves us with the paradigm of human beings as relational beings as God, in Godself, too is relational. This brings us to our next query as to how human beings perceive the "image of God."

Image of God and Disability

Traditionally, in Christian theology, God is understood as transcendent, omnipotent, omniscient and perfect. God's perfection is reflected in human beings. Does that mean only the perfect, the "able-bodied" mirror the image of God? Is it not a one-sided, if not distorted, understanding of God in the Scripture?

God of the Bible is one who suffers, one who is in pain. God's power and transcendence is reflected in terms of weakness. Weakness is not a negative term in the Scripture. "For my power is made perfect in weakness" (2 Cor. 12:9). Gerald F. Moede says, "Surely any Christian theology that cannot come to an understanding of that verse's implications is itself disabled."[13] God's ultimate power is seen on the cross, which from a human point of view is defeat. "Cursed is everyone who hangs on a tree" (Gal. 3:13). His death (weakness) is the ultimate symbol of power. This has implication for our understanding about the image of God. This calls for a rethinking of the image of God—God who is disabled, who is 'weak.' Is disability (weakness) an anathema that cannot be associated with God? What is its implication for Christian theology? Christian theology has largely failed people with disabilities.[14] How and why? Christian theology has largely associated itself with power, dominion and perfection. It, therefore, creates a hierarchical order of creation where imperfection and weakness find no space and are not worthy of preservation and protection.[15] Disability is neither beautiful nor perfect. It is not creative. The disabled are to be "cared for." They cannot contribute. They are not capable of exercising power, perfection, reason and freedom; therefore, they do not reflect the image of God. Historically, Christian faith affirmation has professed and propagated such a theology. Luther and Calvin held people with disability in contempt and justified their removal from society by death as "an act well-pleasing to God."[16] In this sense, Hitler was not so different in his views on the disabled. Do we still carry a similar portrayal of disabled humanity? Stigma and discrimination are part and parcel of our theological formulations. Can we talk of a 'Disabled God' when we discuss human beings created in the image of God? And for PWDs, this theology emerges methodologically from the margins and not from the centre.

Margins?

Theology as a process (or even a construction) involves various sources. NO SOURCES, NO THEOLOGY! However, the question that is raised today is the veracity of the source of the sources, the location of the sources. From where do we gather our sources? Who is the agent of theologising? Has theologising not always been the forte of the privileged, the powerful, the white male, the able, the high caste?

Jenny Daggers and Grace Ji-Sun Kim rightly says:

Theology today is illuminated by a rich vein of theological thinking that has arisen and continues to arise from "peripheral" contexts. This new vein immeasurably enriches the gifts bequeathed to the theological centers that vest their authority in their direct line of descent from the Catholic and Protestant traditions of European Christendom. The well-received categories of received doctrinal traditions take on a new vibrancy as they are turned toward speaking anew the work of the triune God: the creation and redemption of the world is differently known through the lives of its peripheral peoples.[17]

The 'periphery' is challenging the hegemony of the 'centre' (power and privilege) in theology. Margin/periphery has become the centre now. What is a 'margin'? How do we describe such a location?

Daniel Franklin Pilario explains margin in a simple yet powerful manner. He writes:

When we first started to learn how to write, we were trained to write with proper margins: one inch to the right, one inch to the left; more practically measured by the index finger from the edge of the paper, and later folded to make sure the handwritten texts are justified. In a way, the texts, which occupy the centre of the paper were more important. They get the teachers' utmost attention as to form or content. The margins, however, are an empty space. They do not signify anything at all except to be that, an empty space to highlight the text at the centre.

But the margin is also a necessary space. When you write on a card from one end to the other, from top to bottom, without leaving some empty space as margin, it does not quite look good. How many times have we been reprimanded by our teachers to write book reports or formal themes with 'proper margins'? The more spacious the margins, the more pleasant the text appears.

Thus, margins are not entirely useless. They are also fertile grounds for imagination to thrive. When we read books more closely, we want those wider margins as this is where we write our own thoughts, some sort of running commentary or annotation, as it were. Writings on the margins in fact lead us to reader's interpretation of the author's work in another context. In the medieval times, for instance, where monks were mere 'copyists' of sacred books as they could not change the text, they can in fact 'play' with it on the margins. That is why medieval books are filled with lovely, curious or outrageous designs called 'illuminations' that can lead us to the copyist's mind, these being the key to his own interpretation of the central text or of his boredom as he does his lonely job. The margin thus is a space of play to deal with the contingencies, which could not be contained, in the strict logic of life or text inherent of the center.[18]

Margins have two faces. First, it has a passive meaning. They point to some sort of limit, verge, brink, edge or the border of something. It is an empty, non-productive space, often neglected and deserted. It is a passive reality that merely exists to highlight 'the centre.' It is the centre's task, therefore, to 'master' its margins and borders and make them serve its purpose.[19] Recalcitrant margins thus have to be managed and controlled.[20]

However, "margin" is also a dynamic reality. Beyond the notion of limits, margin also refers to "frontiers" (as in "new frontiers of knowledge," "on the verge of discovery" or "cutting edge"). It signifies a dynamic and creative space that has a life beyond what those at the centre can ever imagine. In fact, its presence calls into question the centre's existence. Margin is a space of play but also of resistance for real voices to make themselves heard, neglected or suppressed as they are by the logic of the centre. It is here where life happens with its contingencies and uncertainties, but also with its unexpected disclosures and surprises.[21]

Pilario rightly points out that "margins" should be applied to theology. It should become the privileged locus for theological discourse: the margins of life, the margins of the church, and the margins of society. In these margins, life is revealed in its utter limits. But it is also precisely here, in some special manner, that God chooses to reveal Godself.[22]

However, historically the approach to theology has been undertaken from the centre, not from the periphery or the margins. Interestingly, the biblical mandate for theology is the voices and visions of those who are in the margins. Who are in the margins? Ranjith Guha and Homi Bhabha speak of subalterns. They are of the "inferior rank." They include all those who are suppressed, oppressed, marginalised, pushed out, neglected, left out, rejected, considered incapable and not normal because of their social, financial or physical status.

Margins became the central location of theology only after the arrival of the Latin American liberation theology in the

1960s. It was felt that unless the church, its programmes and its theology turned away from its efforts at self-preservation and lost itself in the margins, it would become irrelevant. Salvation in Christ was now sought in terms of the actual political, economic and social suffering and oppression. Liberation theology paved the way for challenging and displacing the "centre." Margins/periphery becomes the centre now.

There are two fundamental characters of such a theology.

First, it is a theology from the margins. It starts theological reflection and its courses from the experiences of the people in the margins in the belief that their questions have something to tell us about God, about life and the salvation that Jesus proclaims. In fact, we do not evangelise the poor. It is the poor who first evangelises us and calls us to conversion. If there is any theology, it should start with them, with their questions, with their concerns, with their sighs and with their hopes. This is the privileged locus of God's revelation.[23]

Second, theology today ought to be a theology for and with the margins. It is "People's Theology."[24] A people's theology is geared towards the liberation of all. It is in solidarity with those who are in the margins. It is about a "preferential option for the poor and the marginalised." It is a theology *of, with, by, through, from, for* and *in solidarity with* the margins.

Why Margins?

Felix Wilfred opines that the whole biblical revelation points to the fact that God is someone who journeys to the *margins* and is to be found on the periphery (Exo. 3). Anyone who wishes to encounter God will have to migrate to the periphery.[25] The margins is where God encounters people. It is the space of God-visitation. It is where relationships are built.

The Judaeo-Christian God speaks the language of diversity. And the language of the margins is that of diversity. The language of the centre is the language of power—a legitimising power, a manipulative power. God is not a partner to this programme of unity where differences are creased away.

There is a conventional ableist marginalisation of people in the margins because they are not "able to," they are not "normal," they are "different," they are not from "us." Theology means "a discourse on the faith." But who are involved in this theologising? Only the privileged? Wilfred retorts that God is not a partner to such a programme of theologising. God partners with those who are in the margins. There is a preference for those who are in the margins in the *missio Dei*.

Theology is made alive, vibrant, coherent and relevant by the margins. If the margins are the focal point of doing theology, then the sources of theology should and ought to be from the margins. In that sense, it is not a "marginalised" theology, but a theology from the margins.

Disabled God—the 'Marginalised' God

Nancy Eiesland (died at the age of 44 in 2009) was probably the best thing to happen to disability studies from a Christian perspective. In her celebrated work, *The Disabled God: Toward a Liberatory Theology of Disability* (1994)[26], she envisions God as a disabled God. She writes:

> But my epiphany bore little resemblance to the God in a sip-puff wheelchair, that is, the chair used mostly by quadriplegics enabling them to manoeuvre by blowing and sucking on a straw like device. Not an omnipotent, self-sufficient God, but either a pitiable, suffering servant. In this moment, I beheld God as a survivor, unpitying and forthright. I recognized the incarnate

> Christ in the image of those judged "not feasible," "unemployable," with "questionable quality of life." Here was God for me.

She had come to believe that God was in fact disabled. She describes the scene in Luke 24:36-39 in which the risen Christ invites his disciples to touch his wounds.

> In presenting his impaired body to his startled friends, the resurrected Jesus is revealed as the disabled God. God remains a God the disabled can identify with. He is not cured and made whole; his injury is part of him, neither a divine punishment nor an opportunity for healing.

"Disabled God" is a powerful metaphor to understand human beings as the image of God and our knowledge of the image of God. Eiesland rightly argues that disability is not to be seen as a distortion of the image of God, but rather as human beings reflecting the disabled image of God. The disabled body of a human being is a powerful image. It has the potential to help us move out of the confining images of bodily perfection and unity inherent in patriarchal religious doctrines by representing us with a new image of a disabled God. It can provide us with the foundation for a relational model of cooperation based on the ongoing renewal of beloved creation. Valuing the disabled body presents opportunities for people with disability as well as the 'able-bodied' to re-examine their beliefs by learning how disabilities provide positive aspects of our embodiment. Stigma and discrimination can be removed only if we see ourselves created in the image of God who is disabled. Disability envisages a life in relationship with God and other creatures. Such an image of God reflected on human beings can bring a wholesome understanding of the image of God.

Jürgen Moltmann uses the image of the "crucified God" to express this Christological suffering love of God. But the same reasoning also leads to the image of the "disabled God." Jesus on the cross is God disabled, made weak and vulnerable to worldly powers because of the perfection of divine love.

Dietrich Bonhoeffer powerfully expresses the vulnerability of divine love:

> People go to God when [God] is sore bestead, find [God] poor and scorned, without shelter or bread, whelmed under weight of the wicked, the weak, the dead; Christians stand by God in God's hour of grieving. God goes to everyone when sore bestead, feeds body and spirit with [God's] bread; for Christians, pagans alike, [God] hangs dead, and both alike forgiving.[27]

The image of a disabled God reminds us that, in Bonhoeffer's words, the God we know through Christ "is sore bestead . . . poor and scorned." It reminds us that, from a Christological perspective, God's perfection, God's goodness and God's identity are so far from transcending the suffering of the world that he participates deeply and unavoidably in that very suffering.

There is another sense in which the "disabled" image helps us to think about God, particularly about the nature of God's power. Our tendency is to think of divine power in the same terms as our power, except to extend God's power unlimitedly. That is, there are limits to our power; there are no limits to God's power. If we can do some things, God is able to do anything. Thus, human "ableness" provides us with the image to think about God's power. In this context, the image of a disabled God is not simply a shocker but also a theological reminder that we are not to think of God's power or abilities as simply an unlimited extension of our powers or abilities. "Disabled" as an image of God jars us out of our tendency to conceive God as "unlimitedly" able. It reminds us to think of God's power Christologically—God's being with us, suffering with us, broken for us. Of course, God is with us in a way that "ables" us to sustain ourselves, affirm ourselves, and vitalise ourselves towards increasing compassion, creativity and richness of life. But that is a far cry from thinking of God as being able to do whatever God pleases.

Endnotes

[1] Samuel George, "Introduction," in *Christian Theology: Indian Conversations*, ed. Samuel George and P. Mohan Larbeer (Bangalore: BTESSC, 2016), vii.

[2] Ibid., ix.

[3] John Macquarrie, *Principles of Christian Theology*, 2nd ed. (New York: Charles Scribner's Sons, 1977), 1.

[4] Quoted in Alister E. McGrath, *Christian Theology: An Introduction*, 3 ed. (Oxford, U.K. & Malden, U.S.A.: Blackwell Publishing Ltd., 2003 [2001]), 139.

[5] Panikkar writes, "There are not three realities: God, Man, and the World; but neither is there one, whether God, Man or World. Reality is cosmotheandric. It is our way of looking that makes reality appear to us at times under one aspect, at times under another. God, Man, and World are, so to speak, in an intimate and constitutive collaboration to construct Reality, to make history advance, to continue creation." Raimundo Panikkar, *The Trinity and the Religious Experience of Man, Icon-Person-Mystery* (London: Darton, Longman and Todd, 1979). Quoted in http://www.raimon-panikkar. org/english/gloss-cosmotheandric.html (accessed October 09, 2016).

[6] Roger Haight, *Dynamics of Theology* (Bangalore: Claretian Publications, 2002), 1.

[7] John Macquarrie, *Principles of Christian Theology*, 2nd ed. (New York: Charles Scribner's Sons, 1977).

[8] Daniel L. Migliore, *Faith Seeking Understanding: An Introduction to Christian Theology* (Michigan, Grand Rapids: William B. Eerdmans Publishing Company, 1993).

[9] Ibid., 121.

[10] Dorothée Wilhelm, "Women with Disabilities A Challenge to Feminist Theology. Roundtable Discussion," *Journal of Feminist Studies in Religion* 10, no. 2 (Fall 1994): 107.

[11] Migliore, *Faith Seeking Understanding: An Introduction to Christian Theology*, 122.

[12] Ibid.

[13] J. Robert Nelson, "Challenging 'Disabled Theology,'" *Christian Century* 98, no. 39 (December 1981): 1245.

[14] Jeff Hittenberger and Martin William Mittelstadt, "Power and Powerlessness in Pentecostal Theology. A Review Essay on Amos Yong's *Theology and Down Syndrome: Reimagining Disability in Late Modernity*," *Pneuma* 30 (2008): 139.

[15] A. Wati Longchar, "Culture, Sin, Suffering and Disability in Society," in *Embracing the Inclusive Community: A Disability Perspective*, ed. A. Wati Longchar and R. Christopher Rajkumar (Bangalore: BTESSC/SATHRI, NCCI & SCEPTRE, 2010), 73.

[16] Quoted in ibid., 75.

[17] Jenny Daggers and Grace Ji-Sun Kim, eds., *Christian Doctrines for Global Gender Justice* (New York: Palgrave Macmillan, 2015), xi.

[18] Daniel Franklin Pilario, "Doing Theology from the Margins: Experience and Reflections," http://www.svst.edu.ph/doing-theology-from-the-margins.html (accessed October 05, 2016).

[19] Ibid.

[20] cf. Nation-states; for instance, have to always control their borders. Conformity to the pure tradition is another such instance of control.

[21] Pilario, "Doing Theology from the Margins: Experience and Reflections."

[22] Ibid.

[23] Ibid.

[24] I have elsewhere explained the importance of People's Theology. Cf. Samuel George, "Among the People: A Search for People's Theology," in *Among the People: Essays in Honour of Rev. Dr. P. G. Vargis*, ed. V. D. John and Viju Wilson (Delhi: ISPCK & SALT DC, 2012), 184-193.

[25] Felix Wilfred, *Margins: Site of Asian Theologies* (Delhi: ISPCK, 2008), xi.

[26] Nancy L. Eiseland, *The Disabled God: Towards a Liberatory Theology of Disability* (Nashville: Abingdon Press, 1994).

[27] Burton Z. Cooper, "The Disabled God," *Theology Today* 49, no. 2 (July 1992): 176.

Chapter 4

Reclaiming Christ: A Disability-Informed Reading of Christology

The Lord spoke to Moses, saying: "Speak to Aaron and say: 'No one of your offspring throughout their generations who has a blemish may approach to offer the food of his God. For no one who has a blemish shall draw near, one who is blind or lame, or one who has a mutilated face or a limb too long, or one has a broken foot or a broken hand, or a hunch back, or a dwarf, or a man with a blemish in his eyes or an itching disease or scabs or crushed testicles. No descendants of Aaron the priest who has a blemish shall come near to offer the Lord's offerings by fire; since he has a blemish, he shall not come near to offer the food of his God.... But he shall not come near the curtain or approach the altar, not profane my sanctuaries; for I am the Lord; I sanctify them.'" (**Lev. 21: 16-23**)

"... I will save the lame and gather the outcast, and I will change their shame into praise and renown in all the earth." (**Zeph. 3:19**)

Jesus answered, "Neither this man nor his parents sinned; he was born blind so that God's works might be revealed in him." (**John 9:3**)

The three cardinal values in the theme chosen for the WCC Assembly held at Busan, South Korea, in 2013 were Life, Justice and Peace. Dr Olav Fykse Tveit, general secretary of the WCC, rightly asserted that "seeking justice and peace is a call to unity—and may be clearly interpreted as such."[1] Only believing and trusting in the God of life would make this possible. The theme is about both an affirmation and responsibility: The affirmation that God is the God of life and our responsibility to seek justice and peace for all humanity.

A life-affirming God calls us to justice and peace for all, to all. Nothing in the created order is as segregated as human beings. We are segregated in terms of gender, class, colour, creed, caste and abilities/disabilities. To affirm God as the life-giver is to work towards justice and peace, and that is not possible until every human being finds a place in the kingdom of God (where there is justice and peace). Unfortunately, people with disability have found themselves segregated and ostracised because of their physical deformities. How can we talk about life, justice and peace when people with disabilities struggle for their life itself?

This essay is an attempt to understand Christian theology (Christology) and disability from the perspective of the chosen theme of WCC.

The following life story will put into perspective our discussion on disability and theology (Christology):

Satish Gujral, one of India's most renowned artists, lost the ability to hear at the age of eight (he was administered a suspect medicine by a doctor for an injury to the leg). He says "it was a devastating handicap," but in some ways he credits it for his remarkable rise as a leading painter, sculptor, architect and designer of his time. When he met his "normal" (future) wife Kiran, her parents vehemently opposed the marriage. He says, "Like parents anywhere, they wanted her to be married to a normal person." In 1989 he received cochlear implants, which brought back his "ability" to hear. However, this "ability" aggravated things. He explains, "It was like a bomb exploding in my head. I can't fully explain what I felt. My palette changed. Both my sculpting and my painting had a different sense of colour and form." Two years later, he chose to remove the implant, a decision that was reinforced by his wife's support. "I asked her how she felt now that I couldn't hear again, and she replied, 'For me you were never deaf.'" Satish feels his hearing condition has never hindered his enjoyment of life. He says, "I watch movies. Even if there aren't any subtitles, I am able to catch the meaning."[2]

Defining Disability

Disability (as an academic discourse) is a new arrival in academic humanities.[3] It focuses on the disabled body in its manifold locations in time and space: the history of disability, the metaphysics or theologies that attempt to place deviant bodies in a cosmic order, the social construction of disability by the able-bodied and the lived experience of people with disabilities. Since disability studies emerged from comparative literature and contemporary sociology, the focus of major works in the field has been upon the modern era. The medical model of disability, which dominated the nineteenth and early twentieth century thought about disability, viewed it simply as a biological condition to be cured, if possible. The result of this emphasis was that persons with disability were confined to the home and institutionalised. In recent decades, activists and scholars have instead proposed a social-functional model of disability. This approach draws a distinction between the biological conditions and a lack of fit between a given body type and built social structures. Thus, a sensory deficit is called *impairment*. The term *disability* refers to functional limitations that result from the combination of impairment and the social environment.[4]

In defining disability, it is difficult to accommodate the expectation of all disability groups. Disability signifies what a person suffering impairment cannot be and cannot do.

Earlier we have noted how Helander provided the simplest and perhaps the first definition of a disabled person: "A person who in his/her society is regarded as disabled, because of a difference in appearances and/or behaviour."[5]

Because cultures define their norms of being and doing differently, disability is a relative term. Disability may be identified by appearance (ugliness, albinism, the absence of a digit—even a functionally unimportant one), and impairments (mild to moderate mental retardation, club foot) that are recognised as disabling in Western cultures are often not treated as disabling.[6]

The Persons with Disabilities (Equal Opportunities, Protection of Rights and Full Participation) Act, 1995, defines a disabled person as one who suffers not less than forty per cent of any disability as certified by a medical authority.

The term disability, in its attempt to group people with different characteristics perceived to have related or similar effects on human life, is a creation of modern society. The dictionary meaning of disability is "the condition of being unable to perform as a consequence of physical or mental unfitness." The Judaeo-Christian tradition, surprisingly, did not have this type of classification because it described individuals as suffering from specific infirmities; this explains why this term was not included in the Bible.

There are various other terms used to refer people with disability: impaired, handicapped, differently-abled. These definitions often fall under two main classifications, the medical model and the social model. Caregivers, health workers and academics have largely embraced the medical model, while persons with disability, in their lobbying, are largely proponents of the social model.

The Indian Context

India, with over one billion people, is a country with the second largest population in the world. It is estimated that over 70 million people in India live with some kind of disability,[7] giving it the dubious distinction of being the largest geographical concentration of disabled persons on this planet.[8]

According to the 2001 Census, however, there are over 21 million persons with disabilities in India, 2.13 per cent of the total population. This includes persons with visual, hearing, speech, locomotor and mental disabilities. Seventy-five per cent of persons with disabilities live in rural areas, 49 per cent of the disabled population is literate and only 34 per cent of disabled people are employed. It is also estimated that there are over 9.3 million women with disabilities, constituting 42.46 per cent of the total disabled population in India.[9] Women with disabilities are in a more precarious condition, requiring protection against exploitation and abuse. It should be noted that the above-mentioned figures may not provide a true picture of PWDs in India because statistics from the United Nations suggests that 7-10 per cent of the world's population have some form of physical or mental disability.[10]

Considering the economic and social condition of the nation it is almost impossible to cater to the needs of the disabled in

India. In India, positive discrimination for disabled people lags a long way behind that for the Scheduled Castes and the Scheduled Tribes.[11] In India's social welfare agenda, poverty, caste and gender push disability to the bottom of the list. This low priority can be explained by the political weakness of disabled people due to the perceived high economic costs and minimal political benefits of a state response.[12]

The population of disabled persons living under the poverty line shows their condition in India. In rural areas, most disabled persons manage their livelihood by begging.[13] Things are not any better in the urban set-up. PWDs are a great economic and emotional burden to parents and guardians. Lalitha Sridhar says: "Indians spend over 72 billion rupees per annum in caring for their disabled family members. The government bears only a fraction of this cost."[14] With the magnitude of the problems of our variously disabled added to the unemployment levels and underdevelopment among the "normal" and our limited resources spread over numerous pressing demands, the funds that we can spare for the rehabilitation of the severely disabled are likely to remain relatively small for quite some time. The inevitable conclusion from the estimates of the disabled population in India is that we will not be able to treat and rehabilitate even one hundredth of this population institutionally for the next decade or two.[15]

Such is the stark reality of the disabled in India. They are ostracised socially, financially, physically and even religiously. Their voice is the voice of the marginalised. What is the position of religions, especially that of Christians, in this context? Deborah Creamer rightly points out that religion has tended to ignore disability, and the field of disability has paid scarce attention to religion or religious communities. She says, "The church has often been unhelpful and even harmful, as it has related to people with disabilities."[16] Nancy Eiseland writes, "The persistent thread within the Christian tradition has been that disability denotes an unusual relationship with God and that the person is either divinely blessed or damned."[17] Creamer writes, "Historically disabilities have been looked at as symbols of sin (to be avoided), images of saintliness (to be admired), signs of God's limited power or capriciousness (to be pondered), or suffering personified (to be pitied)—very rarely were people with disabilities considered first as *people*."[18] These religious metaphors have been used to legitimise the marginalisation of the disabled in all religious traditions. Christianity is not immune from this process. Our effort in this paper is to understand the relationship between Christology and disability, and its implication for theological discourse.[19]

Christology and Disability: Weakness of God Personified

A Roman Catholic woman working as an assistant in a *L'Arche*[20] community in Belfast in Northern Ireland expressed her fear of living in the midst of a war between Catholics and Protestants. As a Catholic woman, she was terrified to go out on the streets of Belfast. If she went out alone, she would be in genuine danger. However, what she said was profound:

> "When I am with people with profound developmental disabilities I can go anywhere and say anything. The barriers come down on both sides of the divide, Protestant and Catholic. Wherever they go, they seem to bring peace and reconciliation and if I am with them, I can share in that peace. You know, I sometimes wonder if Jesus had Down's syndrome."[21]

She was serious. She was not using metaphorical language; her question was wistful but genuine. Her encounters with people with profound developmental disability had changed the way she saw the world and the ways in which she understood God to be at work in the world. Gone were images of God as the harbinger of liberation and peace through God's great power and might. Instead, the possibility of God being very different from assumed norms, incarnating God's self within the body of a person with Down's syndrome, opened up new vistas of hope, reconciliation and revelation. Because she had entered into relationships with people who have profound developmental disability and allowed those relationships to challenge the way in which she viewed herself, God and the world, the suggestion of a Jesus with Down's syndrome was neither shocking nor outrageous. Why should it be? Nowhere in the Scripture are we told what Jesus looked like, what his IQ was or why people ridiculed him. We simply assume that Jesus looked "something like us." Why do we construct an image of Jesus that is able-bodied and able-minded? Why do we explicitly or implicitly assume that disability is inequitable with the divine image?

Jesus, perfect man though he was, understood disability through bitter experience. Carrying the burdensome cross on the way to his execution, Jesus publicly stumbled and fell—a humiliation many of us "differently-abled" are all too familiar with. It is here that we should reinterpret the idea of "perfection." A Christological dimension of "perfection" leads us to an entirely "different" and "hidden" dimension of God.

The sufferings of Christ, including his death on the cross, are not unrelated to his life lived for others. It is precisely Christ's willingness to go to the cross that shows that he meant what he taught. But in the life of Christ, we can see that God's love finds its perfect expression in suffering love. It should be noted here that all suffering is not suffering love, but a life formed by love for others inevitably leads to one's own suffering, and this is true in Jesus' life and in the history of God.[22]

Jürgen Moltmann uses the image of the "crucified God" to express this Christological suffering love of God. But the same reasoning also leads to the image of the "disabled God." Jesus on the cross is God disabled, made weak and vulnerable to worldly powers because of the perfection of divine love.

Dietrich Bonhoeffer powerfully expresses the vulnerability of divine love:

> People go to God when [God] is sore bestead, find [God] poor and scorned, without shelter or bread, whelmed under weight of the wicked, the weak, the dead; Christians stand by God in God's hour of grieving. God goes to everyone when sore bestead, feeds body and spirit with [God's] bread; for Christians, pagans alike, [God] hangs dead, and both alike forgiving.[23]

The image of a disabled God reminds us that, in Bonhoeffer's words, the God we know through Christ "is sore bestead. . . poor and scorned." It reminds us that, from a Christological perspective, God's perfection, God's goodness and God's identity are so far from transcending the suffering of the world that he participates deeply and unavoidably in that very suffering.

There is another sense in which the "disabled" image helps us think about God, particularly about the nature of God's power. Our tendency is to think of divine power in the same terms as our power, except to extend God's power unlimitedly. That is, there are limits to our power; there are no limits to God's power. If we can do some things, God is able to do anything. Thus, human "ableness" provides us with the image to think about God's power. In this context, the image of a disabled God is not simply a shocker but also a theological reminder that we are not to think of God's power or abilities as simply an unlimited extension of our powers or abilities. "Disabled" as an image of God jars us out of our tendency to conceive God as "unlimitedly" able. It reminds us to think of God's power Christologically—God's being with us, suffering with us, broken for us. Of course, God is with us in a way that "ables" us to sustain ourselves, affirm ourselves and vitalise ourselves towards increasing compassion, creativity and richness of life. But that is a far cry from thinking of God as able to do whatever God pleases.

A Christological perspective to disability helps us to see a "hidden" dimension of God: a suffering God in the weakness of Jesus. It motivates us to view disabilities not as problems to be solved, but rather as particular ways of being human which need to be understood, valued and supported. PWDs are to be welcomed and accepted as people with gifts who have divine dignity, meaning and purpose. Life, justice and peace is only then possible.

Theological Community's Response
- Attitudinal change. Sensitivity to the needs and aspirations of PWDs. Not charity, but equal partners in the pursuit of truth, justice and peace.

- Rethinking of religious/theological categories of sin, salvation, perfection and power.

- Accessibility—disabled-friendly environment. Theological community has to be a welcoming community both in words and deeds. Physical structures can sometimes be rejective and unwelcoming.

- Workshops at the grassroots level. Pastors and lay communities have to be conscientised.

- Practical suggestions to the able-bodied community.

- More literature from the local context—both positive and negative stories to conscientise people.

Endnotes

[1] http://www.oikoumene.org/en/news/news-management/eng/a/article/3591/2013-assembly-theme-g.html (accessed September 01, 2012).

[2] Shashi Sunny, "Sounds of Silence," *People* April 6, 2012, 104-106.

[3] Rebecca Raphael, "Things Too Wonderful: A Disabled Reading of Job," *Perspectives in Religious Studies* 31, no. 4 (Winter 2004): 399.

[4] Ibid.: 400.

[5] Quoted in Bupinder Zutshi, *Disability Status in India- Case Study of Delhi Metropolitan Region* (New Delhi: PhD Centre for the Study of Regional Development, Jawaharlal Nehru University, September 2004).

[6] Susan Erb and Barbara Harriss-White, *Outcast from Social Welfare. Adult Disability, Incapacity and Development in Rural South India* (Bangalore: Books for Change, 2002), 4.

[7] Lalitha Sridhar, "70 million disabled in India, and only 2% are educated and 1% employed," *Infochange*, (September 30, 2010). http://infochangeindia.org/2003060269/Disabilities/Features/70-million-disabled-in-India-and-only-2-are-educated-and-1-employed.html (accessed 30 September 2010).

[8] Erb and Harriss-White, *Outcast From Social Welfare. Adult disability, incapacity and development in rural South India*, p.xii.

[9] India Office of the Registrar General & Census Commissioner, http://censusindia.gov.in/Census_And_You/disabled_population.aspx (accessed September 30, 2010).

[10] Lynda Katsuno and Arne Fritzson, "Disability," in *Dictionary of the Ecumenical Movement*, ed. Nicholas Lossky et al., WCC Publications, Geneva, 2002, p.326.

[11] Erb and Harriss-White, *Outcast from Social Welfare. Adult disability, incapacity and development in rural South India*, p.xiii.

[12] Samuel George, "Persons with Disablties in India," in *Persons with Diabilities in Society: Problems and Challenges*, ed. Wati Longchar and Gordon Cowans (Manila, The Philippines: ATESEA, 2007), 34.

[13] There are instances where the family members of the disabled force them to beg and earn their livelihood.

[14] Sridhar, "70 million disabled in India, and only 2% are educated and 1% employed."

[15] Jainendra Kuman Jha, ed., *Encyclopaedia of Social Work,* Institute for Sustainable Development, Lucknow, 2001, p.208.

[16] Deborah Creamer, "Theological Accessibility: The contribution of disability," *Disability Studies Quarterly* 26, no. 4 (Fall 2006). http://www. dsq-sds.org/article/view/812/987 (accessed September 29, 2010).

[17] Nancy L. Eiseland, *The Disabled God: Towards a Liberatory Theology of Disability* (Nashville: Abingdon Press, 1994), 70-71.

[18] Creamer, "Theological Accessibility: The contribution of disability."

[19] Elsewhere I have tried to explain disability from mission, unity and theological perspective. Cf. Samuel George, "Voices and Visions from the Margins on Mission and Unity: A disability-informed reading of the Pauline metaphor of the church as the body of Christ." *International Review of Mission* 100, no. 1 (April 2011): 96-103; Samuel George, "Image of God and Disability, Stigma and Discrimination," in *Sprouts of Disability Theology* ed. Christopher Rajkumar (Nagpur, India: NCCI, 2012), 60-65.

[20] The L'Arche communities are an international network of inclusive communities within which people with developmental disabilities live together with people who do not have such disabilities. L'Arche is founded on the Beatitudes, and in particular Jesus' teaching that the person who is poor in what society generally values is, in fact, blessed and has deep gifts to offer. L'Arche began in 1964 when Jean Vanier and his spiritual director Father Thomas Philippe, invited two men with profound developmental disabilities, Raphael Simi and Philippe Seux, to come and share their life in the spirit of the gospel and of the Beatitudes. From this first community born in France and rooted in the Roman Catholic tradition, communities have been developed across the globe, the ethos being to share in the lives of people with developmental disabilities in the spirit of the Beatitudes.

[21] John Swinton, "The Body of Christ Has Down's Syndrome: Theological Reflections on Vulnerability, Disability, and Graceful Communities," *Journal Of Pastoral Theology* 13, no. 2 (September 2003): 75-6.

[22] Burton Z. Cooper, "The Disabled God," *Theology Today* 49, no. 2 (July 1992): 176.

[23] Ibid.

Chapter 5

Resurrected (yet) 'Disabled' Christ: Resurrected Body and Disability

In Christendom, resurrection is considered a state of perfection devoid of any "defects." This notion of "perfection" in the resurrected state has adversely affected our Christian understanding of disability. Renowned gospel singer Jim Reeves sang (and we sing): "Across the bridge there's no more sorrow. Across the bridge there's no more pain. The sun will shine across the river. And you'll never be unhappy again."[1] Disability is seen as imperfect and defected and, therefore, it does not have a place in holy places. There is an eternal hope that "across the bridge," this imperfection or defect will not be there. There is a hope of an eschatological healing. Resurrection or afterlife is seen as a state of perfection. And Christians look forward to that state of perfection.

This notion of resurrected body as "perfect" and without defect is contrary to the state to which Jesus was resurrected. His wounds were still visible (and felt) even in the resurrected state. So, if the resurrected Christ has the wounds (symbol of defect) still visible, then why the emphasis on perfection (without defect) in the current state of our life? Why is disability seen as the effect of sin/curse, an imperfection?

This raises fundamental questions about perfection, resurrection and Christology. Here, in this chapter, a humble attempt is made to look at the question of the resurrected body and disability Christologically.

Resurrected Body in the Christian Tradition

The Christian hope of resurrection requires that the one raised be the same person who died.[2] Candida Moss in her lecture "Heavenly Bodies: What does it mean to be Resurrected from the Dead?"[3] rues that even though the writings of the early church and Jesus' tradition talk about resurrection, there is very little exploration into the nature of resurrected bodies. This "lack of interest" in the resurrected body has led to much speculation in our theologising and spirituality. Deformity and imperfection are incompatible with the resurrected body. Out of this speculation arose the notion that (some Christian thinkers thought) it did not make sense to depict the resurrected body as feminine. Women who are resurrected are made whole by being given masculine bodies.

Some of these ideas are borrowed from ancient 'pagan' and Greek backgrounds. Among the Greeks there was an idea that the shape of a person existed even after their body decayed. It is from this view the ritual perfection of cremation emerged. The body needed to be buried intact, with the bones in place, lest this affect the body in the afterlife.

Another perspective that was prevalent made it to the present Christian spirituality in a dominant manner: eschatological healing, or the idea of the dismembered/deformed body being restored to "perfection" by God in an afterlife. The resurrected bodies as heavenly bodies or "perfected" bodies communicate something about the relative values placed on gender, disability and non-disability. In the early church, the resurrected bodies reinscribed culturally dominant norms that, from a disability perspective, were ableist in nature. They present a vision of a future in which the identities of existing bodies—actual people—will be reconfigured "perfectly"; where individual identities will be overwritten, and differences will be eradicated form the heavenly kingdom.[4]

The Christian understanding of resurrected bodies is dominantly influenced by the theology of Paul (cf. 1 Cor. 15). It speaks of resurrected bodies being like Christ's (the first one to be resurrected); resurrected bodies will not be "flesh and blood" (as it is in the present). It will have continuation as well as discontinuation with the old body, like a seed to a plant. He offers a glimpse of that life with the description of the risen body as a spiritual body (*soma pneumatikon*). What is sown perishable, in dishonour, in weakness and as a physical body (*soma psychikon*) is raised imperishable, in glory, in power and as a spiritual body (1 Cor. 15:42-44). He is not speaking about the composition of a body, whether earthly or heavenly, but of different "temporal modes" of existence; a *soma psychikon* is a type of person subject to sin and appropriate to "this age" in contrast to a *soma pneumatikon* which is a type of person transformed by the Spirit and fitting for "new creation."[5] According to Moss, Paul is talking about embodiment.[6] For him, the spiritual body does not deny physicality, but it does tell us that the future body is different from the present. We are yet unaware of the "material" of the spiritual body.

The early Christians were content with the resurrected body of Jesus with scars, but for the general resurrection of the believers (at the end) they believed that disability would be removed from the world. The Christian understanding of resurrected bodies took concrete shape in the post-apostolic period, especially within the context of the intellectual challenges from Greek philosophies. Resurrection became the litmus test for orthodoxy in the early church. Ignatius of Antioch and Justin Martyr (*De Resurrectione*) were among the early thinkers to write on resurrection from a Christian perspective. One finds similarities between these perspectives and that of Paul, especially the notion of continuity as well as discontinuity. To the Graeco-Roman ideas that the characteristics of a person's body are important for his/her identity even after the body itself has died, pseudo-Justinian positions vociferously counter:

> ... For if on earth He healed the sicknesses of the flesh, and made the body whole, much more will He do this in the resurrection, so that the flesh shall rise perfect and entire. In this manner, then, shall those dreaded difficulties of theirs be healed.[7]

Resurrected bodies will be "whole" and "perfect". Disability is not a part of someone's identity; it is part of the irrelevant corrupt matter that is discarded in resurrection. Eschatological cleansing will transform the body so that it is no longer decaying and useless.[8] Irenaeus argued that Jesus healed and raised people from the dead in order to demonstrate that in the afterlife too, God would heal people in their bodies. He reinforces the New Testament connection between healing and salvation, able-bodiedness and divine order. Accordingly, the continued presence of disability in the world is an indication that salvation is incomplete. Therefore, disability is a corruption—a hindrance to finding God. Human identity, as a reproduction of the divine image, is only fully present in the non-disabled. For Irenaeus, disability is the sinful residue that tarnishes God's highly refined and polished creation.[9] Augustine insists that anything "naturally present" in human bodies will be present at the resurrection, but this will not include "deformity" and "infirmity."[10] At the resurrection, the body will be perfectly subject to the soul; mortality, sickness and pain will be replaced by incorruptibility.[11] There is an erasure of deformities in the eschaton.

Cues from the Resurrected Body of Jesus

John 20:24-29 has this uniquely surprising story of the resurrected Jesus with wounds/scars. Scholars point out that they are part of the resurrection apologetics who also point out that John's Gospel is a gospel of exaltation. The story of the resurrection should, therefore, be viewed from the perspective of Jesus being exalted through resurrection.

Thomas decided, "… Unless I see the mark of the nails in his hands, and put my finger in the mark of the nails and my hand in his side, I will not believe" (v.25). Jesus said to Thomas, "Put your finger here and see my hands. Reach out your hand put it in my side" (v.27).

Paul argued (1 Cor. 15) that every resurrection (after Easter) is patterned after the resurrection of Jesus. Our resurrection, like Christ's, entails both continuity and radical transformation that is a new creation; it is creation, however, not from nothing (*ex nihilo*) but from the old (*ex vetere*) matter of this present age.[12] In that case, we need to address some of the questions being raised about the resurrected body of Jesus. What kind of body did he have (and will we have)? Did he have the same physical pre-Easter body? If so, why was the "wound" still visible on his resurrected body? If eschatological healing is what we all look for (in the resurrection body), then what about the body of the resurrected Jesus? For John, it was more a scar than a fresh wound. A scar that is visible and felt. Two aspects can be construed from this passage for Christological and disability studies.

1. Disability studies tell us that if impairments are integral for recognising Jesus, then it is integral for everyone else.

2. It is an anti-Docetist affirmation. The body of Jesus is important. "Mark of the nail" and to touch him is to prove that he is not a ghost.

Yes, we do agree that removal of physical infirmities was one of the outcome/purposes of the coming of the kingdom of God in Jesus, the Christ. However, the perpetuation of the idea of resurrected bodies without infirmities is similar to the idea of the gospel of Thomas where a perfect resurrected body must be male ("for every female who makes herself male will enter the kingdom of Heaven").

Scars on the resurrected body of Jesus debunks this notion (of physical perfection in the afterlife). Infirmity is part of our identity. The scars of the wounds Jesus endured in his body are his identity. He retained his scars lest he be not recognised by those who have seen and experienced him. But could they not have recognised him through other means?

Implications for Disability Theology

Disability theologian Nancy Eiseland was an embodied being and her disability was an integral part of who she was. To the suggestion "Don't worry about your suffering now—in heaven you will be made whole" she wondered: "My disability had taught me who I am and who God is. What would it mean to be without this knowledge? Would I be absolutely unknown to myself in heaven, and perhaps even unknown to God?"[13]

Redefining Perfection (strength, healing)

PWDs are made to feel that their impaired/disformed bodies are 'not perfect.' They are the outcome of sin, a curse ("… who sinned, this man or his parents, that he was born blind?"). This notion of disability as imperfect (therefore sinful/cursed) has impacted the lives of PWDs so negatively that even religion does not help them in any way. A disability-inspired reading of the Bible helps us to relook some of these negative notions.

God's idea of perfection differs from ours. God's perspective on perfection is succinctly portrayed in his chiding of prophet Samuel when he went to choose the new king of Israel. "Do not look on his appearance or on the height of his stature, because I have rejected him; for the Lord does not see as mortals see; they look on the outward appearance, but the Lord looks on the heart." (1 Samuel 16:7)

The scar on the resurrected body of Jesus suggests that disabled bodies are still vehicles of God's glory and resurrected life. Shiao Chong writes, "If the resurrected Jesus is the ultimate image of God (Col. 1:15), and he bears the marks of impairment, then people with disabilities are also fully image-bearers."[14] Eiesland too says that the resurrected Jesus' impairment marks reveal "the reality that full personhood is fully compatible with the experience of disability."[15]

The question of perfection also raises the question of healing. What is healing? What if one is not healed here but there is hope of an eschatological healing?

Mark 9:43-48 talks about being deformed in the kingdom of God. "… It is better for you to enter the kingdom of God with one eye than to have two eyes and to be thrown into hell" (9:47). According to the above passage, if amputees (being deformed and therefore a symbol of sin and curse) can enter the kingdom of God, does it mean that disability and deformity too will inherit the kingdom? This passage alludes to disability in the hereafter. There is no eschatological healing as promised in our theology and spirituality. There is a continuation of what is here and now in the afterlife. Mark subverts the idea that 'able' and 'beautiful' are virtuous. He insists that deformities enter heaven, whereas the 'beautiful' and 'whole' are cast into hell. In the divine scheme, the unnatural becomes natural. Amputation (deformity) in earthly life will save from eternal damnation. If so, where is the question of the disabled being damned?

'Disabled' Jesus: a Christology of Solidarity

The 'Disabled Jesus' is contextual Christology. Eiseland writes,

> It is contextualised in that the disabled God emerges in the particular situation in which people with disabilities and others who care find themselves as they try to live out their faith and to fulfil their calling to live ordinary lives of worth and dignity.[16]

It is at the resurrection that the disciples understood the significance of the person of Jesus. Eiseland further writes:

> In the resurrected Jesus Christ, they saw not the suffering servant for whom the last and most important words was tragedy and sin, but the disabled God who embodied both impaired hands and feet and pierced side and the *imago Dei*. Paradoxically, in the very act commonly understood as the transcendence of physical life, God is revealed as tangible, bearing the representation of the body reshaped by injustice and sin into the fullness of the Godhead.[17]

The resurrection of Jesus points to the incarnational promise that he is the Emmanuel (God with us and will be). He is with us as we are, incorporating the fulness of human contingency and an ordinary life into God. The impaired resurrected body of Jesus points to the fact that the resurrected Christ is revealed as the disabled God. This has implications for our salvation too. The resurrected Christ calls his followers to recognise in the marks of impairment their own connection with God, their own salvation.[18] The resurrection of Jesus does not posit that suffering and loss are triumphantly eradicated, but rather that they are transposed into the promise of a fullness yet to come.[19]

The resurrected body of Christ is not merely a resuscitated or reanimated physical corpse. Neither is it an apparition or some spiritualised and fleshless pseudo-body. It is a transcendent body, appearing and disappearing abruptly. But it is the body of Jesus. He appears bearing wounds from the cross. His risen body demonstrates the extent to which God affirms the created and whole person. Thomas E. Reynolds writes,

> Liberation for new life confirms the goodness of creation, the goodness of the *imago Dei* in its embodied form, but it does so by transforming it into a heavenly form. Hence, redemption is not *from* bodily existence, but *for* bodily life in all its capacities—that is, creativity, relationality, and availability—the richest possibilities of which lie in communion with God.[20]

On the cross, Jesus subjects himself to disability, and his resurrected body continues to bear the scars as a sign of God's solidarity with humanity. His disabled body represents one who understands by embodying disability even in his transformed, resurrected body. It also suggests that disability indicates not a flawed humanity, but a full humanity. Our bodies participate in *imago Dei* in and through vulnerability and its consequent impairments, not despite them.[21]

The resurrected Christ thus embodies the blessed contingencies and dependencies of human life and places these in the heart of God. The impaired body of Christ is an icon of the disabled God, a God whose vulnerability is thus palpably real.[22]

The resurrected Christ as disabled challenges the 'suffering servant model' and the 'conquering Lord model.' It means moving away from the vision of redemption and promised new life in terms of homogeneity, wherein all people are normalised according to the ideal non-disabled body. Jesus' risen body marks God's identification with human vulnerability such that differences are confirmed rather than pressed into a ghost-like conformity. There is no assimilation into normalcy in the new life to come. Of course, we will all be transformed and changed (1 Cor. 15:51), the sting of suffering taken away in a way that we cannot imagine. Even so, we shall remain who we are, not standardised and folded into a homogenised common stock.[23] The resurrected body of Jesus also makes possible a renewal of hope for PWDs, not a utopian hope (of erasure of all human contingency) but a recollection and projection that even our non-conventional bodies, which oftentimes dissatisfy and fail us, are worth the living.[24] Ehrman writes:

> The resurrection brings the harvest of our life—experiences, history, virtues, memories—to a new bodily pitch in Christ. We enter into a new situation of God's love that is continuous yet discontinuous with the former situation. In the resurrection, we shall finally be in our element and in action, transformed in God's love and grace.[25]

The resurrected body of Jesus also points to the acceptance of the disabled God who enables PWDs in finding peace and reconciliation with their own bodies and Christ's body, the church. The impaired resurrected body of Jesus alludes to the fact that disability becomes a new symbol of wholeness and a symbol of solidarity.[26]

Conclusion

The Asian context is predominantly the context of poverty, religious plurality, caste discrimination and gender inequality. It is also the context of extreme ableism. In such a context, Jesus, as the resurrected (yet) disabled Christ, becomes paradigmatic for Christologising. He stands in solidarity with the disabled even in the resurrected state.

The portrayal of a 'disabled' Jesus Christ provides a provoking yet powerful image for Christologising in the Asian context. He is the 'Human One' who identifies with the sufferings of the marginalised, the *ochlos* (the masses). Such an image would inspire us and energise us to imagine and provoke a commitment and conviction to walk with Jesus. This Christology is done by getting involved in the struggles of the people and experiencing the suffering of the people as God's son did on the cross; and in his resurrected form, he bear the marks of that suffering. In and through his life, ministry, death and resurrection the 'disabled' Jesus Christ identifies with the suffering humanity. This Christology, therefore, is not triumphalist, interventionist or imperialistic, but inclusive and challenging.

An attempt was made to understand the resurrected body of Jesus and its implications for disability theology. Two things become clear: the question of eschatological healing is to be rethought and the resurrected Christ stands in solidarity with PWDs. This has serious significance for our theologising and spirituality, which is predominantly based on an 'ableist' ideology. The resurrected Christ calls us again to "put your finger here and see my hands; reach out your hand put it in my side." It is in that 'touch' we experience healing, wholeness, liberation and transformation. And it is in that 'touch' Jesus' resurrection finds its meaning and purpose, i.e., he lived, died and rose again to be in solidarity and communion with humanity, the disabled humanity.

Endnotes

[1] Cf. Revelation 21:4.

[2] For more, Terrence Ehrman, "Disability and Resurrection Identity," *New Blackfriars* 96, no. 1066 (November 2015): 723-738.

[3] https://www.youtube.com/watch?v=hOCQJt92ScE&feature=youtu.be (accessed November 06, 2018)

[4] Candida R. Moss, "Heavenly Healing: Eschatological Cleansing and the Resurrection of the Dead in the Early Church," *Journal of the American Academy of Religion* 79, no. 4 (December 2011): 993.

[5] Cf. Andrew Johnson, "Turning the World Upside Down in 1 Corinthians 15: Apocalyptic Epistemology, the Resurrected Body and the New Creation," *The Evangelical Quarterly* 75, no. 4 (2004): 291-309.

[6] Moss, "Heavenly Healing: Eschatological Cleansing and the Resurrection of the Dead in the Early Church," 993.

[7] On the Resurrection, ANF 1:344.

[8] Moss, "Heavenly Healing: Eschatological Cleansing and the Resurrection of the Dead in the Early Church": 1005.

[9] Ibid., 1008.

[10] *City of God*, 22.20.1152.

[11] Ibid., 22.21.

[12] John Polkinghorne, "Eschatology Credibility: Emergent and Teleological Processes," in *Resurrection: Theological and Scientific Assessments*, ed., Ted Peters, Robert J. Russell and Michael Welker (Grand Rapids, Michigan: William B. Eerdmans Publishing Company, 2002), 50.

[13] Nancy Eiesland, "Encountering the Disabled God," *The Other Side* (September & October 2002), 12-13. http://www.dsfnetwork.org/assets/Uploads/DisabilitySunday/21206.Eiesland-Disabled-God.pdf (accessed November 10, 2018).

[14] Shiao Chong, "The Disabled Savior," *The Banner* (March 3, 2017), https://www.thebanner.org/features/2017/03/the-disabled-savior (accessed November 10, 2018).

[15] Nancy L. Eiesland, *The Disabled God: Towards a Liberatory Theology of Disability* (Nashville: Abingdon Press, 1994), 100.

[16] Ibid., 98.

[17] Ibid., 99-100.

[18] Ibid., 100.

[19] Thomas E. Reynolds, Vulnerable Communion: A Theology of Disability and Hospitality (Michigan: Brazos Press, 2008), 206.

[20] Ibid., 207.

[21] Eiesland, The Disabled God: Towards a Liberatory Theology of Disability, 101.

[22] Reynolds, Vulnerable Communion: A Theology of Disability and Hospitality, 208.

[23] Roy McCloughry and Wayne Morris, Making a World of Difference: Christian Reflections on Disability (London: SPCK, 2002), 73.

[24] Eiesland, The Disabled God: Towards a Liberatory Theology of Disability, 103.

[25] Ehrman, "Disability and Resurrection Identity," 738.

[26] Eiesland, The Disabled God: Towards a Liberatory Theology of Disability, 101.

Chapter 6

Disability Ethics:
Search for a 'Different' Paradigm
in Christian Social Ethics

Introduction

In this chapter, I suggest that a disability perspective offers a valuable dimension to Christian social ethics. This dimension is particularly important as it utilises markedly different premises leading to different conclusions. It is often found that voices and opinions of the disabled are not given proper credence. Christopher Newell opines that the lived experiences of those who identify as disabled is often rejected as emotional or anecdotal. That their knowledge is rejected can easily be demonstrated through an examination of genetics, euthanasia and biotechnology.[1]

In providing such a perspective it needs to be acknowledged that there is no **one** disability voice that can be presented with respect to Christian social ethics. What Newell writes is of equal importance to Christian social ethics too:

> For all of the claims that bioethics listens to many different voices, the social account of disability—an account that claims that disability is more than individual pathology—also reveals a bioethics that either rejects the voices at the margins of able-bodied society, or uses them for the various agendas of bioethics, only to put the disabled voices back on the shelf where they can no longer be heard.[2]

The attempt here is to offer a 'different' account of Christian social ethics from the vantage point of knowledges that are rejected. I do agree to what Newell says:

> … Disability is often central to many bioethical debates, it is also marginal in terms of any acknowledgement of the voices of people with disability. At its best, a social account of disability is a marginal part of the international bioethics' communities, including regulatory bodies and professional practice. In part, this no doubt reflects the disadvantaged structural position of disability in society.[3]

The chapter attempts to "define" or to "do" Christian social ethics from a disability perspective in the Indian context.

Ethics

What is ethics? Is it a moral decision or an analysis of behaviour(s)? Is it *dharma* (duty)?

Many have tried to explain ethics. Normally, the examination and study of morality is referred to as ethics.[4]

Normative ethics is the attempt to identify norms, or standards, of right or good behaviour. In simple terms, it is the attempt to answer Socrates' question: "How should I behave? What should I do? What sort of person should I be?"[5] These questions are answered by presenting arguments and explanations, by appealing to certain norms or standards and explaining why the appeal to these particular norms is appropriate.[6]

Robin Gill writes, "It is concerned with examining the nature of prescriptive language, the grounds on which moral beliefs are held, the types of argument which those who hold them use to promote them, and the consequences that they involve."[7] There is a systematic decision-making in ethical analysis.

Etymologically the word ethics is derived from Greek: verb *eiōtha* and noun *to ethos*, meaning "dwelling" or "stall." The Latin translation for *ethos* is *mos*, from which the word 'morality' is derived. It is an intellectual 'discipline' rather than a 'science.'

Ethics and Morality

Are they similar? Is there a relation between the two?

Ethics had to do with 'stability' or 'stall'; that is, the stability and security that are necessary if one is going to act at all. The Greek term, meaning *to ethos*, was used for animals, not humans—it was necessary that animals be put somewhere for shelter and protection, and "*to ethos*" is the stability and security provided by a "stall" or "dwelling" for animals. The word *eiōtha* (Greek) means, "to be accustomed to" or "to be wont to."

The relationship between stability and custom was an elemental datum of experience. It was the primary office of custom to do for people what the stall did for animals—to provide security and stability.[8] Diogenes Laertius speaks of ethics as that part of philosophy which has to do with "life and with all that concerns us." It is concerned with the foundations of human behaviour, morality with actual practice and behaviour based on these foundations.[9]

Behaviour according to Custom vs Behaviour according to Reflection

"Morality" (*Sitte* in German) gradually came to be understood as behaviour according to custom and "ethics" (*Ethik* in German) as behaviour according to reason or reflection upon the foundations and principles of behaviour or guidance of behaviour (*Tugendlehre* in German).[10]

Ethics is concerned with that which holds human society together. It is the 'cement' of human society, providing the stability and security indispensable to the living of human life.[11]

What is Christian about Ethics?

What does Christianity add to ethics? How does "Christianity" qualify ethics?

As noted above, any ethical attempt to identify the characteristics of a life worth living and examines and articulates standards to inform and guide us in shaping our actions and character is called normative ethics. Christian ethics undertakes the same task with reference to Jesus, the man from Nazareth.[12] The historical figure of Jesus is of utmost importance for ethics to be qualified as Christian ethics. The starting point for Christian ethics is the confession that Jesus is the Christ and that in him, in his works and words, and in the suffering love of his cross, God is present in a special way; that God did not abandon him in the grave but vindicated him and raised him from the dead. The starting point of Christian ethics must always consider what God has done in human history through Jesus Christ.[13] Jesus is authoritative for Christian ethics.

Wayne G Boulton, Thomas D. Kennedy and Allen Verhey write, "Christian ethics reinterprets what is going on here, somehow interjecting the person of Jesus Christ into the relationship between the moral agent—the person doing or feeling something, and the moral patient—the person who is the recipient of the action or feeling."[14] In Christian ethics, Jesus is always in the middle.[15]

Secular ethics identifies the primary questions of ethics as: "What is the good life? What is a life worth living?" The primary questions of Christian ethics are: "Who am I as a follower of Jesus? What life is worthy of one who recognises the authority of Jesus? What sort of people should those who confess Jesus as Christ be?"[16]

Boulton, Kennedy, and Verhey write:

> Christian ethics is the careful, systematic examination of how the life and person of Jesus Christ should impinge upon our moral lives, of who we should be and what we should do in light of what Jesus reveals to us about God and the cause of God. Christian ethics is the disciplined attempt to explain what the significance of morality is for Christians and to identify those norms which should inform and guide the Christian in his or her way of living towards the world.[17]

For Paul L. Lehmann, Christian ethics, properly regarded, has to do with the systematic reflection on what is involved in the ethical nature of Christian religion. It is a reflective analysis, rather than trying to prescribe how Christians ought to behave. The aim of Christian ethics is to rethink what the Christian faith implies, with regard to their behaviour, for those who accept and undertake to live by that faith.[18]

Christian ethics, as a theological discipline, is the reflection upon the question and its answer: What am I, as a believer in Jesus Christ and as a member of his church, to do? To undertake the analysis of this question and its answer is Christian ethics.[19]

Sources of Christian Ethics

No theology, or for that matter ethical analysis, can function without emerging from some source. For our purpose we propose the following sources of Christian ethics.[20]

Experience

It is a matter of fact that some experiences of the life of faith precede theology and may indeed be said to motivate it. Our experience of the life of faith comes, in turn, from participation in a community of faith. Experience is always varied. However, for ethical positioning, experience—either of an individual or community—is extremely essential. At the same time, there is a danger of basing ethics on experience alone. They can easily become distorted by the particular type(s) of experience from which they come. Also, individual idiosyncrasies can turn into universal spiritual principles. Yes, it is true that without experience ethics is abstraction. But basing only on it can make it subjective, introspective and individualistic. However, an ethical approach from the perspective of disability would prioritise the lived experiences of PWDs.

Revelation

In theological formulations, this is the primary source. It has a gift-like character. In the revelatory experience, the holy 'breaks in,' and this 'breaking in' is from "beyond human" to human.

Revelatory experiences can take various forms: natural phenomena, history, personal relationships. In some cases, it is entirely interiorised, and the holy is encountered in the depths of the human mind itself. In Christianity, the person of Jesus Christ is the bearer of revelation.

A basic pattern runs through almost all revelatory experiences: a mood of meditation or preoccupation, the sudden "breaking in" of the holy presence often symbolised in terms of the shining of a light; a mood of self-abasement[21] in the face of the holy; a more definite disclosure of the holy—perhaps the disclosure of a name or of a purpose or a truth of some kind;[22] and the sense of being called or commissioned by the holy to a definite task or way of life.

There is an intrinsic relationship between 'revelation' and 'experience.' Revelation is a mode of religious experience, while our experience of the holy as judging, assisting, addressing and the like all have some revelatory element.

In the construction of any ethical analysis, a proper balance must be maintained between 'experience' and 'revelation.' It is the present experience within a community of faith that gives rise to theology (or ethics) and that enables us to recognise the primordial revelation as revelation. To ward off the dangers of subjectivism, the varieties of experience within the community must be submitted to the relatively objective content of the classic revelation on which the community is founded.

Tradition

Roman Catholics believe that the revelation in Christ has been transmitted to us both in scripture and tradition, while Protestants acknowledge the '*sola scriptura*' position. Tradition always has had its place in helping determine the doctrine and practice of the Christian community. It is no rival to scripture, but is its necessary complement. Scripture is not a frozen record, but something that comes alive only in the ongoing life of the community that first gave birth to scripture and has since proclaimed and interpreted the teaching of scripture. There are ample evidences in the Bible to maintain this: the earliest scriptures were preceded by and based upon tradition (cf. I Cor. 11:23; 15:3) and Jesus was recalled not in scripture, but through the sacraments (cf. I Cor. 11:24).

It was the community of faith that decided the Canon—the decision was based on interpretation of traditions. Doctrines and praxis that were obscure were interpreted in the light of tradition. Scripture needs tradition to guard against private interpretation of the scripture. So, tradition is important for Christian praxis.

Scripture

Scripture is the sacred writings of the community of faith. It provides for the community a kind of memory from which it can recall its past. It is not in itself the revelation but is one important way by which the community of faith keeps open its access to that primordial revelation on which the community has been founded. The scripture, in conjunction with a present experience of the holy in the community of faith, comes alive and renews for us the disclosure of the holy, which was the content of the primordial revelation. This power of bringing again or re-presenting the disclosure of the primordial revelation so that it speaks to us in our present experience is what is meant as what we say 'inspiration.'

The scripture(s) of a community are a major factor in maintaining stability and a sense of continuing identity in the community. It is therefore said that scripture becomes the norm in the theology of a community. So is the ethical positioning of a community. In the Christian community, any theology and ethical stand that claims to be Christian must maintain close and positive relations with the Bible. *The Christian revelation comes in a person, not in a book.* Christian ethical discussions that are biblically based need to be aware of the following two important aspects:

- Misuse of the scripture should be avoided at all cost.

- Awareness of the canonisation process of the scripture.

Culture

Culture refers to the cumulative deposit of knowledge, experience, beliefs, values, attitudes, meanings, hierarchies, religions, notions of time, roles, spatial relations, concepts of the universe and material objects and possessions acquired by a group of people over many generations through individual and group effort. In its broadest sense, it is cultivated behaviour; the totality of a person's learned and accumulated experience which is socially transmitted, or behaviour through social learning.[23] Theology is an intellectual discipline also and it should be expressed "in the clearest and most coherent language available." If theology is to be intelligible, it has to use the language of the culture within which it is undertaken. No one can escape the mentality or intellectual climate of his/her own culture.

The work of theology needs to be done again and again, for its formulations are culturally conditioned and therefore need reinterpretation as cultural forms change. So is the ethical positioning of a community that is both culturally conditioned and entrenched.

However, there is always the danger of overestimating culture for ethical propositions. Theologians/ethicists may try to be modern for the sake of modernity. The need is to find a fine balance between the two extremes of either rejecting or accepting culture uncritically. But it is an inescapable factor.

Reason

Immanuel Kant observed: "Were biblical theology to determine, wherever possible, to have nothing to do with reason in things religious, we can easily foresee on which side would be the loss; for a religion which rashly declares war on reason will not be able to hold out in the long run against it."

Reason can be divided into two broad categories: **speculative reason** and **critical reason**.

Speculative reason further can be divided into: *apriori* (involving deductive reasoning from a general principle to a necessary effect; not supported by fact/derived by logic, without observed facts), and *aposteriori* (involving reasoning from facts or particulars to general principles or from effects to causes/ derived from observed facts).

Critical reason is divided into elucidatory (reason sifts, analyses, expounds, brings into light the content of the revelation), and corrective reason (is directed upon the revelation, questioning its credentials, submitting it to scrutiny and criticism, removing from its content whatever may be involved in irreconcilable conflict with other well-founded convictions that may be held).

If reason is not given its due place in theology, there is the danger of revelation becoming superstition. And overemphasis of reason can lead to subordination of revelation to reason and abstract rigid theories.

The survey of the sources of ethics helps us understand the complexities of ethical analyses. Exaggeration of one or other source would lead to distortions. Ethical analyses, therefore, must hold a fine balance between these sources. A dialogical approach between various sources would lead to a holistic ethical standpoint.

Disability Defined (Clarified)

The concept of disability and the idea that 'the disabled' might form a distinct group is historically recent. The genesis of the idea is intricate but there are evidences to show that they developed primarily for administrative reasons, in parallel with the establishment of residential institutions for disabled people who were unable to contribute to the industrialised workforce or (perhaps more significantly) were considered to hamper their families' productivity.[24] It was also closely connected with the growing standardisation of the body through advances in medical science, and especially to medicine's ability to define standards in quantitative terms.[25]

Until recently, the prevailing framework for understanding disability and what to do with this understanding was provided by the medical model in which disability is a nominative pathology; it is a disease, degeneration, defect or deficit located in an individual. More specifically, it is defined as impairment. The limits of what is considered to be disease, degeneration, deficit or defect are decided by reference to a biomedical norm. The medical model is a binary one that opposes a standard of normative embodiment against every other models of understanding disability. In opposition to the medical model arose the social models of disability. These arose out of dissatisfaction with the limitations of a purely medical perspective for comprehending the experience of disability, especially the experience of collective oppression. The social models' most fundamental criticisms of the medical model are that it wrongly locates 'the problem' of disability in the individual and neglects the social and structural. By contrast, a social model sees social, economic and environmental factors as at least as important as biological ones in the construction of disability. The earliest forms of disability theory made a sharp distinction between impairment—an individual biological manifestation, such as hearing loss—and the collective experience of oppression resulting from a disabling society that, for example, considers television subtitling to be an expensive luxury.

As noted earlier, disability studies is comparatively new to the field of social science. It is theorised principally by the disabled scholar Michael Oliver, who proposed the social model of disability. It is fundamentally different from other social sciences as it is informed by disabled people's reflection on their own experience. Disabled people's activism (social model of disability) has influenced the political positions of disability movements, both in the United Kingdom and to a lesser extent in the United States. It has also influenced educational perspectives on inclusion as a whole.

The social model defines disability as the product of specific social and economic structures and aims at addressing issues of oppression and discrimination of disabled people caused by institutional forms of exclusion and by cultural attitudes embedded in social practices.[26] It also differentiates between impairment and disability. According to the World Health Organization (WHO) there is a difference between impairment and disability.

> An abnormality in the structure of the functioning of the body whether through disease or trauma; disability as referred to the restriction in the ability to perform tasks . . ., and handicap as referred to the social disadvantage that could be associated with either impairment and/or disability.[27]

This classification establishes a causal relation between individual impairment, seen as departure from human normality, and disability, seen as restriction in abilities to perform tasks. Therefore, causes of disability are attributable primarily to biological individual conditions that depart from normal human functioning and determine handicap in terms of disadvantage. These definitions, ultimately, not only promote an understanding of disability primarily as individual but also establish a natural cause related to disability and the associated disadvantage.[28]

Even though there is an intrinsic relationship between the individual model (individual 'abnormality', linked to certain inabilities in performing tasks and therefore to disadvantages), and the social model (disability as social construction), the latter is more 'disabling' because it is about attitude.

Oliver maintains that the social model aims primarily at deconstructing and countering the individual model of disability through a perspective situated in the direct experiences and understanding of disability by disabled people themselves. It also aims to address issues of marginalisation, oppression and discrimination while trying to denounce and remove the disabling barriers produced by hegemonic social and cultural institutions.[29]

Oliver's accounts state that the social model "does not deny the problem of disability but locates it squarely within society"[30] and its definition of impairment and disability is an articulation of this perspective. Basically, disability is seen as something imposed on disabled people on top of their impairment by an oppressive and discriminating social and institutional structure.

Thus, impairment is defined as:

> Lacking part or all of a limb, or having a defective limb, organ
> or mechanism of the body; and disability is the disadvantage
> or restriction of activity caused by a contemporary social
> organisation which takes no or little account of people who have
> physical impairments and thus excludes them from participation
> in the mainstream of social activities.[31]

Disability, therefore, is all that imposes restrictions on disabled people and, as such, disablement is nothing to do with the body.[32]

Disablement is instead caused by the oppression of social and economic structures on disabled individuals who are consequently an oppressed group in society. The disabled people's movement in Britain uses the term "disability" not to mean impairment but to refer to the disabling barriers of prejudice, discrimination and social exclusion. The British Council of Disabled People has adopted the following definition:

> Disability is the disadvantage or restriction of activity caused by
> a society which takes little or no account of people who have
> impairments and thus excludes them from mainstream activity.[33]

Therefore, disability, like racism or sexism, is discrimination and social oppression. Disabled people are those people with impairments who are disabled by society.[34]

This separation of impairment and disability is the cornerstone of the social model. Some disability theorists, therefore, focus exclusively on the material basis of a disabling environment and appear to argue that disability would disappear altogether if all structural barriers were to be removed by changing modes of production, architecture, transport and information provision.[35]

More recently, some theorists have pointed to the inadequacies of the social model as well, as they leave untouched the aspects of social relations,[36] and have begun an exploration of more discursive and phenomenological approaches. Mairian Corker and others see a need for a discursive approach, acknowledging that our very ideas about what impairment is are discursively and socially constructed. The discursive turn has criticised social models for continuing to perpetuate binary models and their tendency to homogenise the experience of all disabled people in order to create or enforce a politically desirable coherence. Disability theory has thus benefited from recent feminist thought that highlights the need to differentiate between the political utility of having a universalised category (women, disabled people) and the invalidity of attempting to universalise the experience of all women or disabled people.[37]

Both the social and discursive theories of disability (in contrast to the medical) have been criticised for minimising the genuine pain and disadvantage of some impairments.[38] Some theorists here are turning to a phenomenological approach that tries to understand disability through the lived experience of impairment. Overall then, within disability studies there is a growing awareness of the complexity of subjective experience as individuals stand at the intersection of many different ontological categories, with gender, age, sexuality and class all having their own complex interactions with disability and impairment that create individual subjectivity.[39]

Since our context is India, it is apt to find a contextual definition of disability. According to the Persons with Disabilities Act (Equal Opportunities, Protection of Rights and Full Participation) Act, 1995, a disabled person is one who suffers not less than 40 per cent of any disability as certified by a medical authority. The disabilities identified are blindness, low vision, cerebral palsy, leprosy, leprosy cured, hearing impairment, locomotor disability, mental illness and mental retardation, as well as multiple disabilities.[40]

Disabilit(y)ethics

Is there a study like this? Or it is the ethics of/from the disabled (PWDs), or ethics informed from the disability perspective?

The purpose of the neologism, "DISABILIT(Y)ETHICS", is to understand the intricacies of ethics and disability. Probably the 'Y' (why?) speaks more than just being the conjunction of the two words, disability and ethics. For me the 'Y' (why?) is an important aspect of doing ethics from a disability perspective. It points to 'Y' (why?) an ethical perspective from disability is fundamental for studying Christian ethics.

In this essay, disability(y)ethics would mean ethical imperatives informed of or from disability experiences.

What are disability experiences? As noted earlier, experience forms a fundamental aspect of human ethical behaviour. From a disability perspective, this experience is: of **pain**—mental, physical, emotional; of **fear**—social, religious, cultural; of **exclusion/rejection**—job security, marital status; of **stigma**—religious, social; of **fun**—caricaturing the disabled in language, jokes.

The experiences of PWDs are mostly negative in nature. However, there are people who have turned their negative experiences into positive ones (but they are comparatively fewer).[41]

Why is experience so important for PWDs? They 'see' what others cannot 'see' or experience. It is an experience of intimacy and togetherness, of seeing the particulars and valuing the small or insignificant (which, many a time, the 'abled' gloss over). Every so-called insignificant experience is important for them. It is in the 'insignificant' they 'see' the important.

Now these are the valuable contributions of disabilit(y) ethics towards the sources of doing Christian ethics: fear, stigma, exclusion, intimacy/togetherness and valuing the insignificant.

Issues in Disabilit(y)ethics

This section would delineate a few issues that PWDs face in doing ethics.

Accessibility (structural changes)

Approachability and suitability are crucial issues PWDs face in their mundane life. In a society like India, with extremely limited disability awareness and a high degree of prejudice, the standard of life of PWDs is extremely poor. Most buildings (including educational institutions, religious places and theological institutions) and roads are disabled-unfriendly. Making structural changes is seen a financial 'burden.' Churches and theological institutions are so unwelcoming through the sheer structural set-up itself. Creamer writes, "The church has often been unhelpful and, even harmful, as it has related to people with disabilities."[42] An inclusive approach to structural changes in the building process is a necessary step towards including PWDs as equal partners.

Philanthropic to Accommodation, or Accompanying, model

PWDs are often seen as an object of philanthropy/charity and not equal subjects who can contribute towards society. Accommodation demands acceptance as equals—as human beings created in the image of God.[43] This also addresses the issue of stigma, taboo, discrimination and ostracisation. As noted earlier, disability—like racism or sexism—is discrimination and social oppression. Such a position does not need philanthropy, but accommodation.

Search for a New or 'Different' Language

The lampooning, jeering, discriminatory and sometimes hostile language (calling names, caricaturing, stereotyping, labelling) 'murders' the human in us. Such derogatory language often leaves PWDs in the periphery—s/he has to make the extra effort to reclaim the centre. Acceptance and acknowledgment are tantamount to achievements. Only success stories are recognised, e.g., Dr. Stephen Hawking.[44] The ladder of recognition is to be 'climbed' through the efforts of PWDs themselves, and only then are they recognised. After that they become 'examples,' and 'role models' to be emulated.

Need for Support System

PWDs are dependent on family and friends for economic, physical and emotional needs. They need a support system to ventilate their psychological turmoil—guilt, fear, anger. They need someone to 'cushion' them.

Sin and Disability

The disciples of Jesus asked, "Rabbi, who sinned, this man or his parents, that he was born blind?" Jesus answered, "Neither this man nor his parents sinned; ..." (John 9:2-3). Eiseland rightly points out that "the persistent thread within the Christian tradition has been that disability denotes an unusual relationship with God and that the person is either divinely blessed or damned."[45] Creamer writes, "Historically disabilities have been looked at as symbols of sin (to be avoided), images of saintliness (to be admired), signs of God's limited power or capriciousness (to be pondered), or suffering personified (to be pitied)—very rarely were people with disabilities considered first as people."[46] Disability as a sign of sin raises the question of what sin is.[47] Sin is a denial of our essential relatedness to those who are genuinely 'other.' Migliore writes, "We deny our dependence on the Other who is God and reject our need for our fellow creatures, most particularly those who seem so totally strange and 'other' to us—the victim, the poor, the 'leftover person.'[48]"[49] Should we add to this list the disabled too? In this sense, the disabled are not the sinners (?) but they are victims of sin or they are sinned against. Sin is "the depth of human intolerance for difference." Unless the taboo of 'disability as sin' is removed from our religious thought, PWDs do not see a great future in the church.

Ordination and Disability

People called both inwardly and outwardly by the Spirit of God for leadership responsibilities are set apart by a service of ordination.[50] It is about being faithful to God and to all people of God. Migliore writes, "Ordination is properly understood *missiologically rather than ontologically*."[51] It is a mysterious change in hierarchical status, an elevation over other Christians and an ordination. It is being commissioned and authorised to a particular task in the power of the Spirit. It is in the "jar of clay" we have the treasure (the gospel),[52] says St. Paul. Is not this the truth about human frailty? Rahner points out that this human frailty and weakness is a promise that God's grace is victorious even through the ministry of "frail" and ordinary people.[53]

Migliore writes, "Ordination to ministry of Word and sacrament is *inclusive rather than exclusive.*"[54] No one is to be excluded from the exercise of this office on the basis of any criteria of gender, race, caste and disability. However, historically, Christian ministry has been only for the able-bodied. It is carried out by the able-bodied. Unfortunately, there are some scriptural warrants to maintain this proposition.[55] I have elsewhere explained how the church as the body of Christ constitutes both 'strong' and 'weak' members.[56] Amos Yong states that for the full health and proper functioning of the church, PWDs are indispensable.[57]

Conclusion

Ethics is Christian when attitudes are analysed from the standpoint of Jesus, the Christ. This essay was an attempt towards an ethical proposition that is 'different.' It 'stands' on the lived experience of those who are identified as disabled which is often rejected as emotional or anecdotal. Such an experiential ethical standpoint forms the springboard for disabilit(y)ethics in India. This ethical approach prioritises empathy and concern for the other.

Endnotes

[1] Christopher Newell, "Disability, Bioethics, and Rejected Knowledge," *Journal of Medicine & Philosophy* 31, no. 3 (2006): 269.

[2] Ibid., 270.

[3] Ibid.

[4] Wayne G. Boulton, Thomas D. Kennedy, and Alan Verhey, *From Christ to the World: Introductory Readings in Christian Ethics* (Grand Rapids, Michigan: William B. Eerdmans Publishing Company, 1994), 2.

[5] Ibid., 2-3.

[6] Ibid., 3.

[7] Robin Gill, *A Textbook of Christian Ethics* (Edinburgh: T. & T. Clark Ltd., 1985), 4.

[8] Paul L. Lehmann, *Ethics in a Christian Context* (New York: Harper & Row, Publishers, 1976), 24.

[9] Ibid.

[10] Ibid., 25.

[11] Ibid.

[12] Boulton, Kennedy, and Verhey, *From Christ to the World: Introductory Readings in Christian Ethics,* 3.

[13] Ibid., 4.

[14] Ibid.

[15] Søren Kierkegaard might have put it this way, "Jesus Christ is the 'middle term' in Christian ethics." Ibid., 4.

[16] Ibid.

[17] Ibid., 5.

[18] Lehmann, *Ethics in a Christian Context,* 23.

[19] Ibid., 25.

[20] My theological foundations are very much entrenched in two foundational theological treatises namely: John Macquarrie, *Principles of Christian Theology,* 2nd ed. (New York: Charles Scribner's Sons, 1977), 4-16; Daniel L. Migliore, *Faith Seeking Understanding: An Introduction to Christian Theology* (Michigan, Grand Rapids: William B. Eerdmans Publishing Company, 1993). The sources of ethics are adapted from these books.

[21] Sometimes terror, sometimes consciousness of sin, sometimes even doubt of the reality of the experience.

[22] This element is called the 'content' of the revelation.

[23] http://www.tamu.edu/faculty/choudhury/culture.html (accessed October 24, 2012).

[24] C. Barnes, G. Mercer, and T. Shakespeare, *Exploring Disability: a Sociological Introduction* (Cambridge: Polity Press, 1999), 18-20.

[25] J. Leach Scully, "A Postmodern Disorder: Moral Encounters with Molecular Models of Disability," in *Disability/Postmodernity: Embodying Disability Theory,* ed. M. Corker and T. Shakespeare (London: Continuum, 2002), 48-61. Quoted in Jackie Leach Scully, "Drawing Lines, Crossing Lines: Ethics and the Challenge of Disabled Embodiment," *Feminist Theology:*

The Journal of the Britain & Ireland School of Feminist Theology 11, no. 3 (2003): 266.

[26] Lorella Terzi, "The Social Model of Disability: A Philosophical Critique," *Journal of Applied Philosophy* 21, no. 2 (2004): 141.

[27] Quoted in ibid., 142.

[28] Ibid.

[29] M. Oliver, *The Politics of Disablement* (Basingstoke: Macmillan, 1990), 11.

[30] M. Oliver, *Understanding Disability: From Theory to Practice* (Basingstoke: Palgrave, 1996), 32.

[31] According to The British Council of Disabled People, impairment is a characteristic, feature or attribute within an individual which is long term and may or may not be the result of disease or injury and may 1. affect that individual's appearance in a way which is not acceptable to society, and/or 2. affect the functioning of that individual's mind or body, either because of, or regardless of society, and/or 3. cause pain, fatigue, affect communication and/or reduce consciousness. Quoted in Jenny Morris, "Impairment and Disability: Constructing an Ethics of Care That Promotes Human Rights," *Hypatia* 16, no. 4 (2001): 2.

[32] Oliver, *Understanding Disability: From Theory to Practice,* 35.

[33] Quoted in Morris, "Impairment and Disability: Constructing an Ethics of Care That Promotes Human Rights," 2.

[34] Ibid.

[35] Scully, "A Postmodern Disorder: Moral Encounters with Molecular Models of Disability," 267.

[36] Cf. C. Thomas and M. Corker, "A Journey Around the Social Model," ibid., 18-31.

[37] Scully, "Drawing Lines, Crossing Lines: Ethics and the Challenge of Disabled Embodiment," 267.

[38] Cf. M. Corker, "Differences, Conflations and Foundations: The Limits to 'Accurate' Theoretical Representation of Disabled People's Experience?," *Disability & Society* 14, no. 5 (1999): 627-42; L. Crow, "Including All of Our Lives: Renewing the Social Model of Disability," in *Exploring the Divide: Illness and Disability,* ed. C. Barnes and G. Mercer(Leeds: The Disability Press, 1996), 55-73.

[39] Scully, "Drawing Lines, Crossing Lines: Ethics and the Challenge of Disabled Embodiment," 267.

⁴⁰ Samuel George, "Persons with Disablities in India," in *Doing Theology from Disability Perspective*, ed. Wati Longchar and Gordon Cowans (Manila, The Philippines: ATESEA, 2011 (2007)), 32-33.

⁴¹ A few famous examples are: Fanny Crosby (1820-1915) who became blind in her infancy. She went on to become one of the most prolific gospel song writers (she wrote over 8,000 hymns, 1,000 secular songs) in history. Oscar Leonard Carl Pistorius (1986-) is a South African sprint runner. He has double below-knee amputations and uses prostheses. Currently he is the T44 (single below-knee amputees) world record holder for the 200- and 400-metre events, and was previously the world record holder for the 100 metres as well.

⁴² Deborah Creamer, "Theological Accessibility: The Contribution of Disability," *Disability Studies Quarterly* 26, no. 4 (Fall 2006). http://www.dsq-sds.org/article/view/812/987 (accessed September 29, 2010).

⁴³ I have dealt elsewhere with the issue of disability and image of God. Cf. Samuel George, "Image of God and Disability, Stigma and Discrimination," in *Sprouts of Disability Theology* ed. Christopher Rajkumar (Nagpur, India: NCCI, 2012), 60-65.

⁴⁴ Stephen William Hawking (1942-2018) is a renowned British theoretical physicist and author. He had a motor neurone disease related to amyotrophic lateral sclerosis, a condition that progressed over the years. He was almost entirely paralysed and communicated through a speech generating device.

⁴⁵ Nancy L. Eiseland, *The Disabled God: Towards a Liberatory Theology of Disability* (Nashville: Abingdon Press, 1994), 70-71.

⁴⁶ Creamer, "Theological Accessibility: The Contribution of Disability."

⁴⁷ The Greek word for sin is *hamartia* (missing the mark). Hebrew has different words for the many different forms of sin. The closest to *hamartia* is *hatt't*, which in contrast to '*awon*' (wilful therefore culpable failure to hit the mark) suggests carelessness. Cf. Wolfhart Panneberg, *Systematic Theology*, vol. 2 (Grand Rapids, Michigan & Edinburgh: William B. Eerdmans Publishing Company & T & T Clark Ltd., 1994), 239.

⁴⁸ José Comblin, *Retriving the Human: A Christian Anthropology* (Maryknoll, New York: Orbis Books, 1990), 55.

⁴⁹ Migliore, *Faith Seeking Understanding: An Introduction to Christian Theology*, 130.

⁵⁰ Ibid., 227.

⁵¹ Ibid., 228.

[52] II Cor. 4:7.

[53] Karl Rahner, *Meditations on the Sacraments* (New York: Seabury Press, 1977), 61-62.

[54] Migliore, *Faith Seeking Understanding: An Introduction to Christian Theology*, 230.

[55] E.g., "No one of your offspring throughout their generations who has a blemish may approach to offer the food of his God. For no one who has a blemish shall draw near, one who is blind or lame, or one who has a mutilated face or a limb too long, or one who has a broken foot or a broken hand, or a hunchback, or a dwarf, or a person with a blemish in eyes, or an itching or scabs or crushed testicles ...he shall not come near the curtain or approach the altar, because he has a blemish, that he may not profane my sanctuaries ..." (Lev. 21:17-23).

[56] George, "Voices and Visions from the Margins on Mission and Unity: A disability-informed reading of the Pauline metaphor of the church as the body of Christ," 100-102.

[57] Amos Yong, "Disability and the Gifts of the Spirit: Pentecost and the Renewal of the Church," *Journal of Pentecostal Theology* 19, no. 1 (2010): 86-89.

Chapter 7

Friendship as a Model of Disability Engagement

> Jesus said, "You are my friends if you do
> what I command you. I do not call you servants any
> longer, …; but I have called you friends, because I have
> made known to you everything that I have heard from my
> Father." (John 15:14-15, *NRSV*)

At least in Western societies, the lives of people with disabilities (PWDs) have improved in the last few decades. Many of them have control over their own lives, they have gained in opportunities to participate in society and, more importantly, they are more self-aware. This is not true in the Indian context, but in recent years there have been collective dedicated efforts on the part of the government, civil societies, NGOs, faith communities and others to make the lives of PWDs more amiable.

Important are these victories. However, people with disabilities continue to feel rejected and shunned. Hans S.

Reinders rightly points out the reason for this failure of society to include PWDs as their own. He writes, "… Disabled people are rarely chosen as friends, except by other disabled people."[1] He further points out:

> Friendship is a very rare experience in their lives. People without disability seldom want to become involved, particularly when it takes a strong commitment to do so. They remain ignorant of what it is to live with a disability, and many apparently want to keep it that way.[2]

Since the mid-1970s, the field of disability movement has been dominated by the social model of disability (SMD). The buzzword since then has been *inclusion*. However, a critical relook at it often gives a different reality of inclusion. Luke S. Carlos A. Thompson rightly points out the difficulty with conventional notions and perspectives about inclusion.

> Simple *inclusion* offers minimal to no *lasting* social change or ideological equality. To put it another way, social inclusion requires that public buildings are accessible (ramps, automatic or push-button doors, parking spaces, etc.); that individuals with bodily impairments be considered for employment if task-descript qualifications are met; and, that equal pay be offered for employee competency irrespective of bodily difference. All of these changes in law and policy have greatly improved the living conditions of those with a variety of bodily impairments. However, at its best, this call for social change fails to account for the nuance in life experiences from one form of impairment to the next. At its worst, there is an emphasis upon physical impairments, thus overlooking individuals with intellectual impairments completely.[3]

This offers a serious critique of *inclusion*. It does not necessarily require society to alter its *perception* of or *attitudes* towards human difference. This instead changes to infrastructure, and social policies allow the negative impact of exclusionary misperceptions towards human differences to be less pronounced—not unlike a Band-Aid over a lasting wound. Yes, removing the Band-Aid so that the wound can breathe may be uncomfortable, but it is crucial to the healing process. Emphasising inclusion may get individuals into the building, but inclusion offers little change in the way human difference is *perceived* and *received* by those *already* inside the building.

Responding positively to human difference requires society to see and welcome individuals as *people* first. The second thing that must be done is to consider the individual's unique limitations. *Receiving* human differences within this framework, however, makes note of personal differences in order to see how and where these differences can *belong* within—and therefore, enrich the tapestry of—the societal fabric.[4] Inclusion does not celebrate difference. For that to happen one has to belong. Belonging is not 'being included'. It is different. In order to belong, one needs to be missed if one is not there. If they are not missed, they do not belong; and if they do not belong, there is no true community—for anyone.[5]

This *belonging* can be applied in praxis through *friendship*. Disability is being noticed, welcomed, and accounted for between friends rather than being seen as a disadvantage between unequal individuals. Friendship allows both individuals to contribute to the life and community that both individuals inhabit. In fact, this mutual benefit is such that when persons isolate themselves, the change in the partnership is keenly felt.[6]

PWDs are mostly surrounded by family, caregivers or support workers. These relationships are therefore either a matter of natural necessity or of contractual obligation. Both of these relationships are extremely important for the disabled person. However, neither can establish the one crucial good that disabled people long for—being chosen as a friend. Friendship is unique because it is constituted by appreciation. It is special because it is freely chosen. No other relationships can give what friendship gives.[7]

Friendship liberates and enables all people to live humanly. It is what John Swinton calls "rehumanisation."[8] Friendship does not expect anything even when not reciprocated. This is possible only through interdependence, acknowledgment of limitations as *humans* and a *mutual* sense of belonging. Exclusion of anyone renders true *community* impossible and, therefore, society itself is *incomplete*. What is needed is belonging expressed through friendship. This position acknowledges that the able-bodied need the disabled just as much as the disabled need the able-bodied. The goal of such a friendship model is that there is a fundamental recognition that by excluding the other *both* the able-bodied and the disabled have an incomplete understanding of what it is to be human. Friendship brings out the humanness within everyone involved. This requires that able-bodied individuals recognise the need for those previously deemed to be 'in the margins' to contribute to social norms, culture, religion, spirituality and identity formation.[9] Within this model of disability (friendship model), it is the contribution of the disabled in conjunction with the voice of the able-bodied that equals 'mainstream' society.

Christian Anthropology

Discrimination against (exclusions) PWDs comes from the defective anthropology of all people that hinders understanding of PWDs as equals, thus leading 'us' to avoid a friendship with 'them.'

Genuine friendship with PWDs relies upon a theological account of being human. Unless human life itself is seen as a gift of God and human lives are valued because God has chosen all people including PWDs as 'His' friends, there is no other truly universal account to justify seeing people with disabilities as being on a par with others. Such a positioning of our theology requires a fundamental revaluation of life in a non-hierarchical mode so that proper virtues can be cultivated amidst a human community of equals.

Christian Friendship

Christian friendship is dependent on truthfulness with regard to who we are in relationship to one another. Within these relationships, we must continuously receive the gift of God, but receiving it properly is often the hardest thing to do. Especially in our relationships with people who are utterly dependent, we are tempted to hide ourselves in our own strength. However, God's gift cannot be received in self-possessing strength.[10] Friendship with God is a gift of the Spirit. God's friendship in every instance precedes our friendship with 'Him'. Friendship with PWDs is friendship with God.

Endnotes

[1] Hans S. Reinders, *Receiving the Gift of Friendship: Profound Disability, Theological Anthropology, and Ethics* (Grand Rapids, Michigan & Cambridge, U.K.: William B. Eerdmans Publishing Company, 2008), 4.

[2] Ibid., 4-5.

[3] Luke S. Carlos A. Thompson, "Moving Beyond the Limits of Disability Inclusion: Using the Concept of Belonging Through Friendship to Improve the Outcome of the Social Model of Disability," *International Journal of Humanities and Social Sciences* 10, no. 5 (2016): 1489.

[4] Ibid., 1490.

[5] John Swinton, *Dementia: Living in the Memories of God* (Grand Rapids, Michigan: William B. Eerdmans Publishing Company, 2012), 279.

⁶ Thompson, "Moving Beyond the Limits of Disability Inclusion: Using the Concept of Belonging Through Friendship to Improve the Outcome of the Social Model of Disability," 1490.

⁷ Reinders, *Receiving the Gift of Friendship: Profound Disability, Theological Anthropology, and Ethics*, 4-5.

⁸ John Swinton, *Resurrecting the Person: Friendship and the Care of People with Mental Health Problems* (Nashville: Abingdon Press, 2000), 23.

⁹ Thompson, "Moving Beyond the Limits of Disability Inclusion: Using the Concept of Belonging Through Friendship to Improve the Outcome of the Social Model of Disability," 1490.

¹⁰ Reinders, *Receiving the Gift of Friendship: Profound Disability, Theological Anthropology, and Ethics*, 16.

Chapter 8

Church as Body of Christ: Revisioning Mission and Unity

Introduction

Mission and unity are the inherent characters of the church. However, historically this approach to mission and unity has been undertaken from the centre and not from the periphery or the margins. Interestingly, the biblical mandate for mission and unity comes from the voices and visions of those who are in the margins. Who is in the margins? In this paper we agree with Ranjit Guha's and Homi Bhabha's definition of subalterns. They are of the "inferior rank." They include all those who are suppressed, oppressed, marginalised, pushed out, neglected, left out, rejected and considered incapable or not normal because of their social, financial or physical status. Voice of people with disability are one such neglected voice from the margins. This chapter tries to highlight the potential barriers faced by the disabled both in religious structures, and in scripture and metaphors. It also suggests certain theological possibilities in which disability is not simply a consumer of tradition but rather a constructive element that offers new options for theological refection on mission and unity from the margins.

Why Margins?

Felix Wilfred says the biblical revelation points to the fact that God is someone who journeys to the *margins* and is to be found on the periphery (Ex. 3). Anyone who wishes to encounter God will have to migrate to the periphery.[1] It is in the margins that one encounter God of the Bible. It is the space of God-visitation. It is where relationships are built.

The Judaeo-Christian God speaks the language of diversity. And the language of the margins is that of diversity. The language of the centre is the language of power—a legitimising power, a manipulative power. God is not a partner to a programme of unity where differences are folded away.

A conventional ableist marginalises people with disabilities because they are not "able to," they are not "normal," and they are "different." Mission means "a special assignment given to an individual/group of people." Who is involved in the *missio Dei*? Only the "abled"? Wilfred retorts that to such a programme of mission and unity God is not a partner. God partners with those who are in the margins. There is a preferential option for those who are in the margins in the *missio Dei*.

Voices and Visions of the Margins: The Disabled

This paper is written from the perspective of the Indian context. Its context as explained earlier is one that has not given much importance to disability issues in its national agenda.

Even the definitions of disabled in India can be disabling. In India for all official purposes these are the definitions used:

The Persons with Disabilities (Equal Opportunities, Protection of Rights and Full Participation) Act, 1995, defines a disabled person as one who suffers not less than 40 per cent of any disability as certified by a medical authority.[2]

The National Sample Survey Organisation (NSSO) of India, which conducted surveys of persons in India with disabilities in 1981, 1991 and 2002, considered disability as "any restriction or lack of abilities to perform an activity in the manner or within the range considered normal for human being." It excluded illness or injury of recent origin (morbidity) resulting in temporary loss of ability to see, hear, speak or move.[3]

One can understand why the voices of the disabled in India are so muted and subdued when we understand the context. The reality that disability discourse was given almost negligible status in Indian society can be construed from the fact that the 1981 Census of India was the first and last twentieth century census to enumerate the disabled. In it, they were classified as "blind," "dumb," and "crippled." Extreme criteria of impairment were used in this census. As a result, only 1.1 million were identified as disabled.[4] According to the Census 2001, there are over 21 million persons with disabilities in India, 2.13 per cent of the total population. This includes persons with visual, hearing, speech, locomotor and mental disabilities. Seventy-five per cent of persons with disabilities live in rural areas, 49 per cent of the disabled population is literate and only 34 per cent are employed. It is also estimated that there are over 9.3 million women with disabilities, 42.46 per cent of the total disabled population in India.[5] Women with disabilities are in a more precarious condition. They require protection against exploitation and abuse.

Earlier we had noted that in the social welfare index of India disability issues fare far behind. It is the lowest priority on state welfare agendas. In India's social welfare agenda, poverty, caste and gender push disability to the bottom of the list. This low priority can be explained by the political weakness of disabled people due to the perceived high economic costs and minimal political benefits of a state response.[6]

Poverty and huge population coupled with negligible social security has pushed the disabled population in India to the brink. In rural areas disabled persons mostly manage their livelihood by begging.[7] In the urban set-up, things are not any better. PWDs are a great economic and emotional burden to parents and guardians. Lalitha Sridhar says, "Indians spend over 72 billion rupees per annum in caring for their disabled family members. The government bears only a fraction of this cost."[8] Such enormity is overwhelming for any country especially considering the socio-political-economic context of India. The inevitable conclusion from the estimates of the disabled population in India is that we will not be able to treat and rehabilitate even one hundredth of this population institutionally for the next decade or two.[9]

Such is the stark reality of the disabled in India. Socially, financially, physically and even religiously they are ostracised. Their voice is the voice of the marginalised. What is the position of religions, especially that of Christianity, in this context? Deborah Creamer rightly points out that religion has tended to ignore disability, and the field of disability has paid scarce attention to religion or religious communities. She says, "The church has often been unhelpful and even harmful, as it has related to people with disabilities."[10] Eiseland writes, "The persistent thread within the Christian tradition has been that disability denotes an unusual relationship with God and that the person is either divinely blessed or damned."[11] Creamer writes, "Historically disabilities have been looked at as symbols of sin (to be avoided), images of saintliness (to be admired), signs of God's limited power or capriciousness (to be pondered), or suffering personified (to be pitied)—very rarely were people with disabilities considered first as *people*."[12] These religious metaphors have been used to legitimise the marginalisation of the disabled in all religious traditions. Christianity is not immune from this process. Our effort in this paper is to reread such a metaphor from a disability-informed perspective. This rereading will have ramifications for an inclusive ecclesiology in which persons with disabilities become equal partners in the pursuit of mission and unity of the church.

Disability-Informed Reading of the Pauline Metaphor of the Church as the Body of Christ (1 Cor. 12)

Why a disability-informed reading?[13] What Jennie Weis Block says is important for our consideration for such a reading. She writes:

> [S]criptural exegesis of the disability passages begins with a 'hermeneutic of suspicion,' asking a question not unlike the question posed by many feminist theologians when they inquire if Scripture, with its decidedly patriarchal bias, can be relevant and meaningful to women. Likewise, disability advocates must ask difficult questions such as: Do the Scriptures have an 'ableist' bias that ultimately oppresses people with disabilities?[14]

Dominant hermeneutical structures have neglected the subjective milieu radiating from behind and between the texts. Not only the historical interests of the origin of the text and its original milieu but the relationship between the text and the reader too are very important. The dynamic of the text and its impact on the reader are extremely important in the present context. It is our contention here that experience of disability—and the attendant impact on a human community—is precisely the kind of profound human and religious experience that provides a crucial and religiously fruitful vantage point for biblical interpretation.[15]

Paul in 1 Corinthians 12 discusses the issue of unity and diversity in the body of Christ and its importance to the church. Paul's message of church as the body of Christ is an important aspect, especially when he is facing the stark reality of disunity in the Corinthian community. Unity is the hallmark of the body of Christ; at the same time, unity preserves diversity. All members equally participate in maintaining the unity and the "health" of the body. The most disregarded, despised and marginalised members are essential to the body of Christ. A disability hermeneutic would suggest that the Pauline idea about bodily members that seem "to be weaker" (*asthenestera*, 1 Cor. 12:22) or "less honourable" (*atimotera*) or "less respectable" (*aschemona*, 1 Cor. 12:23) fits the image of people with disabilities. The root word for "less respectable" (*aschemon*) could very well mean "misshapen" or "ugly." Amos Yong argues that while some may object to the interpretation that Paul was referring to members who were physically deformed or crippled, inclusion of people with disabilities in this context in no way does any violence to Paul's rhetoric and fits very well with the overall intent of what he is attempting to do in this passage—break down the elitist, triumphalist and exclusionary attitudes certain Corinthians had developed *vis-à-vis* others in the congregation.[16]

Paul also mentions the weaker or less respectable parts of the body that are necessary and indispensable. It is felt that the body parts in 1 Corinthians 12:15-17, 21 would have been associated with strength by the original readers of the epistle. Yong says:

> A disability perspective would highlight, however, that in the ancient Mediterranean context these bodily parts are the nexuses through which human bodies interface and interact with the world. They are considered to be necessary just because eyes see, ears hear, hands feel, and feet cross the external world. They are strong (not weak) because they are the means through which people discern the world, do things, get around, even protect themselves. The weaker bodily parts, on the other hand, were those members that were 'passive' by contrast—perhaps internal organs of the body in need of protection—not only incapable of acting out the bodily desires and needs but also unable to fend for themselves and hence reliant on those members of the body who were 'stronger.'[17]

Interestingly, if impaired, these necessary parts of the body—hand, eye, foot, etc.—are no longer strong but weak.

Yong is right when he argues that people with disabilities are implicit in this metaphorical discourse about the church. It is also noted that the Spirit distributes gifts liberally and graciously so that people with disabilities are just as capable of contributing to the edification of the community of faith and hence are necessary.[18]

The disability-informed reading of the Pauline metaphor of the body with diverse members (both weak and strong) is interesting because the unity of the body is constituted by its diversity. This has serious implications for our theme of mission and unity of the body of Christ. It is wrought by the amalgamation of both the "abled" and the "disabled." 1 Corinthians 12:14 mentions the diversity of the members in the one body. Yong says, "The one body of Christ has many members, including people across the spectrum of disabilities…. The health of the body requires the working of its many parts: the 'stronger' and 'weaker,' those with more or less honour or respect, with each member recognized and honoured."[19]

Paul is of the opinion that the weaker members are equally necessary for the health of the whole group, but also that it is such marginalised members who are to be given greater honour and granted greater respect (1 Cor. 12:23). What Yong says of this is of great importance:

> From a disability perspective, then, people with disabilities are by definition embraced as central, necessary, and essential to a fully healthy and functioning body of Christ. Beyond such a descriptive statement, however, is the implicit prescription of St. Paul: that 'those members of the body that we think less honourable we clothe [or should and ought to clothe] with greater honour' (1 Cor. 12:22). Thus, it is the responsibility of the whole body to put a stop to the stigmatization and marginalization of people with disabilities.[20]

Paul's major focus while speaking of the church as the body of Christ was to combat factionalism that threatened the Corinthian congregation. He was aggrieved by those elitists and so-called superiors in the church who excluded others who were apparently considered less spiritual and thus threatened to fragment the unity of the body (cf. 1 Cor. 8, 1 Cor. 14). From a disability perspective, Paul's insistence on the unity of the body involving diversity takes on greater significance as diversity includes the weaker ones. It is also interesting to note that Paul's theology of strength resides wholly in his theology of weakness; so his views regarding the strength of the ecclesial body depends wholly on the "weakness" of the bodily members.[21]

The unity of the church is grounded in each person as an indispensable part of the body. Individuality is honoured in that each believer serves the body in a distinct way—neither less nor great. Christian unity neither requires uniformity nor encourages it. For Christians to be different is not only acceptable, but it is expected and even necessary, as explained above, for the richness, wholeness and vigour of the body. Difference is extremely important for the life and survival of those who are in the margins. Abolishing differences and diversity is a programme of domination, whereas affirmation of difference is the way of victims.[22] God is on the side of the "different" and the "weaker." Wilfred says, "The agenda from the periphery (*the margins*) is the agenda of God."[23] The real future of humanity is there, because persons in the margins constantly challenge the established order about its ways of exclusion and strive towards a world of inclusion and justice.

Yong's outline of an inclusive ecclesiology should be considered for our deliberation on mission and unity: voices and visions from the margins. He says:

> [T]he church consists of the weak, not the strong: people with disabilities are thus at the centre rather than at the margins of what it means to be the people of God.... Each person with disability, no matter how serious, severe, or even profound, contributes something essential to and for the body, through the presence and activity of the Spirit. ...
>
> People with disabilities become the paradigm for what it means to live in the power of God and to manifest the divine glory.[24]

Importance of Disability Theology for Mission and Unity

Our deliberations on the metaphor of body make it amply clear that "weaker" members are indispensable for the mission and unity of the church. They are the paradigm for the manifestation of God. Jennie Weiss Block argues that while God cannot be fully known, the lens of disability highlights a God who is unfailingly committed to inclusion and access. She further argues that "the mandate for access and inclusion is biblically based, central to our baptismal promise and commitment, and rooted in the Triune God."[25] For her, "A theology of access is important because the gospel of Jesus Christ is a gospel of access; creating access for those on the margins is a Christian mandate."[26]

God is not incompatible with disability and God is for and on the side of people with disabilities. The Exodus God is the God who is on the side of the marginalised. Such models help explain to churches that they should attend to this issue as an issue of justice, that people with disability too are part and parcel of the church. Unity and mission without the inclusion of their voices and visions is not only a truncated mission endeavour, but is also impossible because God is not a partner to such an endeavour.

Endnotes

[1] Felix Wilfred, *Margins: Site of Asian theologies* (Delhi: ISPCK, 2008), xi.

[2] Samuel George, "Persons with Disabilities in India," in *Persons with Disabilities in Society: Problems and challenges*, ed. Wati Longchar and Gordon Cowans (Manila, The Philippines: ATESEA, 2007), 36.

[3] Ibid.

[4] Ibid., 3.

[5] India Office of the Registrar General & Census Commissioner, http://censusindia.gov.in/Census_And_You/disabled_population.aspx (accessed September 30, 2010).

[6] George, "Persons with Disabilities in India," 38.

[7] There are instances where the family members of the disabled force them to beg and earn their livelihood.

[8] Sridhar, "70 million disabled in India, and only 2% are educated and 1% employed."

[9] Jainendra Kuman Jha, ed., *Encyclopaedia of Social Work* (Lucknow: Institute for Sustainable Development, 2001), 208.

[10] Deborah Creamer, "Theological Accessibility: The contribution of disability," *Disability Studies Quarterly* 26, no. 4 (Fall 2006). http://www.

dsq-sds.org/article/view/812/987 (accessed September 29, 2010).

[11] Nancy L. Eiseland, *The Disabled God: Towards a liberatory theology of disability* (Nashville: Abingdon Press, 1994), 70-71.

[12] Creamer, "Theological Accessibility: The contribution of disability."

[13] For a discussion on disability hermeneutics cf. Kerry H. Wynn, "The Normate Hermeneutic and Interpretation of Disability within the Yahwistic Narratives," in *This Abled Body: Rethinking disabilities in biblical studies*, eds. Hector Avalos, Sarah J. Melcher, and Jeremy Schipper (Atlanta: Society of Biblical Literature, 2007), 91-101.

[14] Jennie Weiss Block, *Copious Hosting: A theology of access for people with disabilities* (New York: Continuum International Publishing Group Ltd., 2002), 101.

[15] Donald Senior, "Beware of the Canaanite Woman: Disability and the Bible," in *Religion and Disability: Essays in scripture, theology and ethics*, ed. Marylin E. Bishop, (Kansas City: Sheed & Ward, 1995), 2.

[16] Amos Young, "Disability and the Gifts of the Spirit: Pentecost and the renewal of the Church," *Journal of Pentecostal Theology* 19, no. 1 (2010), 86-87.

[17] Ibid., 87.

[18] Ibid.

[19] Ibid., 88.

[20] Ibid.

[21] Ibid., 89.

[22] Wilfred, *Margins: Site of Asian theologies*, xvi.

[23] Ibid., xviii.

[24] Yong, "Disability and the Gifts of the Spirit: Pentecost and the renewal of the Church," 89.

[25] Block, *Copious Hosting: A Theology of access for people with disabilities*, 22.

[26] Ibid., 120.

Chapter 9

Theological Education as Missional and Diaconal Formation

Introduction

Martin Kahler wrote, "Mission is the mother of theology… theology as exegesis as its starting point and missionary proclamation as its goal… theology, rightly understood, has no reason to exist other than crucially accompany the *missio Dei*."[1] Rightly so, theological education that does not lead to missional formation is not Christian theology.

In this chapter an attempt is made to understand theological education as missional and diaconal formation from the perspectives of disability studies. Also, here is a brief look at the contributions of the Ecumenical Disability Advocacy Network–World Council of Churches (EDAN-WCC).

Missional Formation?

Lesslie Newbigin wrote:

> The Mission of the church is everything that the church is sent into the world to do: preaching the gospel, healing the sick, caring for the poor, teaching the children, improving international and

interracial relations, attacking injustice. The Missions of the church is the concern that in places where there are no Christians there should be Christians. In other words, Missions means to plant churches through evangelism.[2]

Newbigin adds that the aim of missions should be the establishment of a new Christian community that is as broad as society and is as true to the national situation. He also indicates that fighting against injustices in the world should also be the task of mission.[3] However, because of his emphasis on ecclesia-centric missiology, there is strong criticism that for him mission is Christianisation. It is being rightly pointed out that the 'church-centric' view of mission does not fully correspond with the biblical view of mission.[4] God is the one sending the church. God is the one sent (1 Pet. 2:9). Since there is a new perception of church today, mission is viewed as "God's turning to the world."[5] J.J. Kritzinger points out that mission involves the whole person in her or his total situation in response to the whole gospel.[6] Mission is striving for the kingdom of God.

Emilio Castro states that God's mission and ours is to bring in the "kingdom."[7] The goal of the 'kingdom' is life in its fullness. The 'kingdom' has to do with the welfare of the whole person, not excluding the social, political and economic aspects of life.[8] J. Verkuyl states that the ultimate goal of the *missio Dei* is the 'kingdom of God.'[9] Kritzinger writes:

> We understand Christian mission to be a wide and inclusive complex of activities aimed at the realisation of the reign of God in history. It includes evangelism but is at the same time much wider than that. Perhaps one could say that mission is the 'cutting edge' of the Christian movement—that activist streak in the church's life that refuses to accept the world as it is and keeps on trying to change it, prodding it on towards God's final reign of justice and peace.[10]

Mission, therefore, is God's mission where we (church, society, creation) are in the continuous process of establishing the kingdom of God.

Diaconal Formation?

The term "diakonia" (from the Greek verb *diakonein*, to serve; cf. *diakonos*, male or female servant) refers to service as a permanent activity of the church throughout its history. It is the "responsible service of the gospel by deeds and by words performed by Christians in response to the needs of people"; it is rooted in and modelled on Christ's service and teachings.[11] It is also a consecrated ministry of the church. Diaconal ministers work to seek wholeness in the world and to help the people of God to live out the gospel. They are committed to alerting the church to the needs of the world. It is a ministry of word and service, sharing the hope of Christ, helping where there is need and equipping others for healing and justice in the world. Diaconal ministers serve in and through agencies, institutions (both church-related and secular), traditional church programmes in congregations, synods and the churchwide organisation as they build bridges between the church and the world.[12]

Diakonia, therefore, is service unto humanity as taught and practised by Christ.

Theological Education?

Simply put, it is educating 'people of God' for ministry. It is training men and women to serve God and humanity. It is different from Christian education, which is usually provided in all churches and available for all seekers. Whereas, theological education is not for all, usually results in special service and leadership, and usually takes place in a college/seminary or in a theological education programme beyond ecclesial boundaries.

Is theological education biblically legitimate? Well, Jesus was a theological educator. He was, of course, much more than that but certainly no less. He taught the twelve, and he taught the crowds. The Gospels frequently call him "teacher" or "rabbi," suggestive of the popular reputation he gained for teaching. Indeed, more than once he identified himself as a teacher, confirming the assessment of others: "You call me 'Teacher' and 'Lord,' and rightly so, for that is what I am" (John 13:13; cf. Matt 23:10; 26:18). He "taught" people and they were amazed at his teaching (Matt. 7:28; 13:54; 22:22,33) and delighted in it.[13] Jesus not only taught but commissioned his disciples to "… teaching them to obey everything that I have commanded you" (Matt. 28:20).

Over the years, the meaning and purpose of theological education has evolved. Today, it is not merely an academic pursuit. It is more than just classroom learning. It involves academic learning, training in service and ministry to others and being witnesses (*marturia*) to gospel values. This process of formation ought to pursue new 'paradigms' of theologising where justice and liberation become the defining values. For that to happen, the centre of theologising ought to move to the margins.

'Margin' is a dynamic reality. Beyond the notion of limits, margin also refers to "frontiers" (as in "new frontiers of knowledge," "on the verge of discovery" or "cutting edge"). It signifies a dynamic and creative space that has a life beyond what those at the centre can ever imagine. In fact, its presence calls into question the centre's existence. Margin is a space of play, but also of resistance for real voices to make themselves heard—neglected or suppressed as they are by the logic of the centre. It is here where 'life' happens, with its contingencies and uncertainties, and also with its unexpected disclosures and surprises.[14] 'Centring' theology on the margins, therefore, is a creative and dynamic way of doing theology that is full of surprises.

Daniel Franklin Pilario rightly points out that 'margin' should be applied to theology. It should become the privileged locus for theological discourse: the margins of life, the margins of the church and the margins of society. In these margins, life is revealed in its utter limits. But it is also precisely here, in some special manner, that God chooses to reveal Godself.[15]

However, historically the approach to theology has been undertaken from the centre and not from the periphery or the margins. Interestingly, the biblical mandate for theology is the voices and visions of those who are in the margins. Who are in the margins? They are of the "inferior rank," says Ranjith Guha. They include all those who are suppressed, oppressed, marginalised, pushed out, neglected, left out, rejected, considered incapable and not normal because of their social, financial or physical status. People with Disabilities (PWDs) are one such neglected voice from the margins.[16]

It is often felt that margins became the central location of theology after the arrival of the Latin American liberation theologies in the 1960s. It was argued that unless the church, its programmes and its theology turned away from its efforts at self-preservation and lost itself in the margins, it would become irrelevant. Salvation in Christ was now sought in terms of the actual political, economic and social suffering and oppression. Liberation theologies paved the way for challenging and displacing the "centre." Margins/periphery becomes the centre now.

There are two fundamental characters of such a theology:

First, it is a theology from the margins. It starts theological reflection and its courses from the experiences of the peoples in the margins in the belief that their questions have something to tell us about God, about life and the salvation that Jesus proclaims. In fact, we do not evangelise the poor. It is the poor who first evangelises us and calls us to conversion. If there is any theology, it should start with them, with their questions, with their concerns, with their sighs and with their hopes. This is the privileged locus of God's revelation.[17]

Second, theology today ought to be a theology for and with the margins. It is "People's Theology."[18] A people's theology is geared towards the liberation of all. It is in solidarity with those who are in margins. It is about a "preferential option for the poor and the marginalised." It is a theology *of*, *with*, *by*, *through*, *from*, *for* and *in solidarity with* the margins.

Authentic missional formation is not possible if theological education is not tuned to the realities of the context. Theological education has to take the perspective of the margins to be missionally effective and challenging.

Theological Education from Disability Perspectives for Missional Formation

People with disability are one such neglected voice from the margins. They face barriers both in religious structures, and in scripture and metaphors. Disability theology (theology from the perspectives of PWDs) suggests certain theological possibilities in which disability is not simply a consumer of tradition but rather a constructive element that offers new options for theological refection on mission and unity from the margins.

Wilfred opines that biblical revelation points to the fact that God is someone who journeys to the margins and is to be found at the periphery (Ex. 3). Anyone who wishes to encounter God will have to migrate to the periphery.[19] The margins is where God encounters people. It is the space of God-visitation. It is where relationships are built.

The Judaeo-Christian God speaks the language of diversity. And the language of the margins is that of diversity. The language of the centre is the language of power—a legitimising power, a manipulative power. God is not a partner to a programme of unity where differences are folded away. A conventional ableist marginalises people with disabilities because they are not "able to," they are not "normal" and they are "different." Mission means "a special assignment given to an individual/group of people." Who are involved in the *missio Dei*? Only the "abled"? Wilfred retorts that God is not a partner in such a programme of mission and theologising. God partners with those who are in the margins. There is a preferential option for those who are in the margins in the *missio Dei*.

Disability theology offers a unique hermeneutical tool for doing theology from the perspectives of the margins—PWDs. It is the perspective of forceful marginalisation, humiliation, pain and pathos, disabling, naming, shaming and rejection. It is an experiential theology striving for liberation and justice. It is to this perspective of theologising that EDAN-WCC has contributed immensely.

Ecumenical Disability Advocacy Network–World Council of Churches (EDAN-WCC): Its Contributions towards Missional Formation

The World Council of Churches (WCC) has since the early 1960s treated the issue of disability as an important concern of the Christian church. At the fourth Assembly of the WCC in 1968, an attempt to explore the church as a more inclusive community intensified. All subsequent WCC General Assemblies continued to reflect on the place of persons with disabilities in the church and society and to give direction to ensure that disability remains on the council's agenda.

EDAN was born during the 1998 WCC, the eighth Assembly in Harare, Zimbabwe, when 10 persons with disabilities from different parts of the world were invited to participate as advisers. In their role as advisers, they took the opportunity to deliberate in their own forum on how best to influence churches to recognise and incorporate persons with disabilities in their witness and service programme. It was through this consultation that the advisers decided to form EDAN as a vehicle that would carry WCC's work on disability by giving it a new form that would give it continuity and visibility in churches. The WCC then considered it as a model for work with persons with disabilities and it was adopted as a WCC programme within the Justice, Peace and Creation team. During the restructuring that followed the 2006 WCC Assembly, the ninth one, at Porto Alegre, Brazil, EDAN's work was placed within Programme 2 of Unity, Mission, Evangelism and Spirituality. This has provided an opportunity for it to benefit greatly from the WCC call to churches for visible unity in which all gifts and contributions at the individual level are indispensable for the building of the one church of Christ.[20] The Busan (South Korea) Assembly in

2013 reaffirmed the works of EDAN as central to the mission and purpose of the WCC.

EDAN embarks on a **mission** to "advocate for the inclusion, participation and active involvement of persons with disabilities in all spiritual, social, economic and structural life of the church and society" with a **vision** of "Church of All and for All, an epitome of truly inclusive community."[21]

From its inception, EDAN has prioritised theological education as the area where disability issues will be fostered. In hindsight, one can say that to a great extent they have been successful in integrating disability issues into mainstream theological education. The objective here is aimed at influencing the inclusion of persons with disabilities in these institutions both as students as well as faculty members and, more importantly, at preparing theological students for ministry with and among persons with disabilities as a way to improve the attitudes held by churches and society on persons with disabilities. Today, through the efforts of EDAN-WCC, disability issues are taught in several institutions around the globe. The works of EDAN are divided into various regions: the Middle East (Lebanon, Egypt, Jordan); Caribbean (Jamaica, Haiti, Barbados, Trinidad and Tobago, Cuba); Asia (India, Myanmar, Sri Lanka, Bangladesh, Taiwan, Indonesia, the Philippines, Korea); Latin America (Bolivia, Mexico, Columbia, Argentina, Ecuador); Europe; North America (Association of Theological School, National Council of Churches of USA); the Pacific (Solomon Islands, Tahiti, Samoa, Fiji, Tonga, Cook Island, Davuilevu); Africa (Kenya, Ghana, Congo, Uganda, Tanzania, Zimbabwe, Botswana, Malawi, South Africa, Burundi, Rwanda, Nigeria).

EDAN has been engaged in advocacy for an inclusive community for all with churches from its inception. EDAN and Ecumenical Theological Education (ETE) came to realise that without addressing the issue in theological colleges, it will not have an impact in the life of the church and society. To institutionalise the issue, EDAN and ETE decided to launch a programme on "Disability and Theological Discourse" in 2016. Samuel Kabue, the programme executive of EDAN-WCC, and Wati Longchar,[22] consultant at ETE, initiated several consultations in Asia and the Pacific. The first EDAN workshop in India was held in Bangalore, which was hosted by BTESSC/SATHRI (Board of Theological Education of the Senate of Serampore College/South Asia Theological Research Institute) in 2006. This meeting was indeed a momentous moment in the field of theological education in India. At Bangalore, it was felt that a sustained theological training was necessary for disability issues to become mainstream in the theological and ecclesial community. Therefore, the need was felt to include it in the theological curriculum. Accordingly, two syllabuses for the Bachelor of Divinity (BD) degree programme at the Senate of Serampore-affiliated colleges were proposed and it was accepted in the revised curriculum for BD studies. To accompany theological teachers and students in handling the new curriculum on disability, the second project—"Doing Theology from Disability Perspective"—was initiated, which led to the publication of *Doing Theology from Disability Perspective: A Theological Resource Book on Disability*. EDAN supported the DTh colloquium on "Inclusive Community: Disability Perspective" organised by BTESSC/SATHRI in 2009. The outcome was the publication of another resource book for theological education in India from a disability perspective, *Embracing the Inclusive Community: A Disability Perspective*.[23]

Achievements and Challenges in India

- Within a short period of time, disability issues have found considerable space in the theological discussions under the Senate of Serampore-affiliated colleges. However, very little is achieved in the evangelical theological circles.

- Since 2006, four major theological works have been produced in India from the disability perspective. Since then many students have written BD, MTh, DMin theses from a disability perspective. An anthology on Asian disability theology is being produced. We will need more theological literature in the field of disability theology in India.

- There is a dearth of PWDs who undergo theological education. Structural challenges and attitudinal problems have dampened many potential theological PWD aspirants.

- More theological trainers (both PWDs and others) should be given disability pedagogical training.

Theological Education (Disability Perspective) as Missional Formation

In a recent lecture, Dr. Ravi Tiwari, the former registrar of the Senate of Serampore College (University), reminded us in no uncertain terms: "By design Serampore College is theological, so it is 200 years old not 100 years. Theological education was integral from its inception."[24] He further states: "For [William] Carey, theological education was missional not pastoral. It is therefore, Serampore College was (and ought to be), a missionary college."[25] Similarly, Stephen Bevans writes, "… Any and all theological education at whatever level should be infused with a missionary perspective and be geared to missionary practice… today especially, theological education should be missionary formation."[26]

As noted earlier, there is a tectonic 'paradigm shift' in theological thinking since the emergence of liberation theologies in Latin America. Liberation from injustices have become the matrix of our theologising. Margins (the marginalised) are the new 'centre' of our theologising. This has also affected the mission of the church as "mission *of/by/for* the marginalised." Bevans has rightly pointed out that "… theological education as missional formation must teach theologizing that 'listens to all the voices.'"[27] They have to listen to unusual voices, the voices "beyond the boundaries" and settled notions. In this sense, theological education as missional formation has to listen to the voices, struggles, pains and experiences of the disabled.

Missional education is teaching "missional living." It is pluriform ministry and service, encompassing a full spectrum from careful stewardship of creation, liberation of the marginalised and creating just societies to active evangelistic work as ambassadors of God's reconciling love.[28] Theological education (disability perspective), therefore, strives to establish the kingdom of God (*missio Dei*) where PWDs find their rightful place in theologising and missional living.

How to go about this in missional education? As noted earlier, disability is an experiential theology striving for liberation and justice. EDAN has strived to focus on the missional training of the theological fraternity from this experiential perspective. Since it is a lived theology, the focus is also on a lived missional education. PWDs are no more objects of this missional education, but the subject and initiators. The goal is to embark on a missional journey that would engage, expose (the forceful marginalisation of PWDs through able-bodied theologies) and empower the kingdom of God.

Theological Education (Disability Perspective) as Diaconal Formation

Is theological education only meant for "furtherance" of the spiritual and ritual activities of the church? What about its role in the service of humanity and creation? In what way does theological education become a tool for diaconal formation? Even though the church from its inception has emphasised diaconal ministry (Acts 6:1-7), theological education's formal emphasis was seldom on it. The emphasis on the social model of disability and its overall effects on theological education has paved the way for a re-emphasis on diaconal ministry. Such an education is centred on others' needs and the subject of this education are the marginalised themselves. There is a reversal of role in such an education. The "needs" of the marginalised are not "calculated" or "decided" by those at the centre but by those in the periphery. This kind of diaconal formation has a lasting effect on the ministry of the church. Theological education (disability perspective) helps in reinventing diaconal ministry.

Endnotes

[1] Quoted in David J. Bosch, *Transforming Mission: Paradigm Shifts in Theology of Mission* (Maryknoll, New York: Orbis Books, 1991), 16.

[2] Lesslie Newbigin, "Mission and Missions," *Christianity Today* 4, no. 22 (August 1, 1960): 911.

[3] Ibid.

[4] J. C. Hoekendijk, "The Church in Missionary Thinking," *International Review of Mission* XLI, no. 163 (1952): 332.

[5] Jerry Pillay, "Theological Foundation of Mission," in *Mission Continues: Global Impulses for the 21st Century*, ed. Claudia Währisch-Oblau and Fidon Mwombeki, Regnum Edinburgh 2010 Series (Oxford: Regnum Books International, 2010), 13.

[6] J. J. Kritzinger, *The South African Context for Mission* (Cape Town: Lux Verbi 1988), 34. The terms *kerygma* (preaching), *koinonia* (fellowship),

diakonia (service) in combination describe the main aspects of the witness (*marturia*) and also worship (*leiturgia*) of the kingdom. Quoted in ibid.

[7] Emilio Castro, *Freedom in Mission: The Perspective of the Kingdom of God. An Ecumenical Inquiry* (Geneva: WCC Publications, 1985), 56-60.

[8] Pillay, "Theological Foundation of Mission," 13.

[9] J. Verkuyl, *Contemporary Missiology: An Introduction* (Grand Rapids, Michigan: William B. Eerdmans Publishing Company, 1978), 203.

[10] Nico Botha, K.K. Kritzinger and Tinyiko Maluleke, "Crucial issues for Christian Mission–A Missiological Analysis of Contemporary South Africa," *International Review of Mission* 83, no. 328 (January, 1986): 21-36.

[11] https://www.oikoumene.org/en/resources/documents/wcc-programmes/justice-diakonia-and-responsibility-for-creation/diakonia (accessed June 17, 2020).

[12] https://stpaulcarlisle.org/diaconal-ministry/ (accessed June 17, 2020).

[13] Keith Ferdinando, "Jesus, the Theological Educator," *Themelios* 38, no. 3 (2013): 360.

[14] Daniel Franklin Pilario, "Doing Theology from the Margins: Experience and Reflections," http://www.svst.edu.ph/doing-theology-from-the-margins.html (accessed July 1, 2018).

[15] Ibid.

[16] Samuel George, "Voices and Visions from the Margins on Mission and Unity: A disability-informed reading of the Pauline metaphor of the church as the body of Christ," *International Review of Mission* 100, no. 1 (April 2011): 96.

[17] Ibid.

[18] I have elsewhere explained the importance of People's Theology. Cf. Samuel George, "Among the People: A Search for People's Theology," in *Among the People: Essays in Honour of Rev. Dr. P. G. Vargis*, ed. V. D. John and Viju Wilson (Delhi: ISPCK & SALT DC, 2012), 184-193.

[19] Felix Wilfred, *Margins: Site of Asian Theologies* (Delhi: ISPCK, 2008), xi.

[20] http://www.edan-wcc.org/index.php/about-us/history (accessed January 08, 2016).

[21] http://www.edan-wcc.org/index.php/about-us/who-we-are (accessed 08 January 2016).

²² Dr. A. Wati Longchar in his role as the Consultant ETE and Director in-Charge of BTESSC/SATHRI has played a very crucial role in the introduction and furtherance of disability studies in the Indian theological context.

²³ A. Wati Longchar and R. Christopher Rajkumar, eds., *Embracing the Inclusive Community: A Disability Perspective* (Bangalore: BTESSC/SATHRI, NCCI & SCEPTRE, 2010).

²⁴ Year 2018 is being celebrated as the Bicentennial of the establishment of Serampore College by the 'Serampore tri'—William Carey, Joshua Marshman, and William Ward. It is also being celebrated as the centennial of the establishment of the Senate of Serampore College (University) offering degrees in theology.

²⁵ At the Faculty Retreat of Allahabad Bible Seminary (Serampore), dated 20-21 June 2018.

²⁶ Stephen Bevans, "Theological Education as Missionary Formation," in *Reflecting on and Equipping for Christian Mission*, ed. Stephen Bevans et al., Regnum Edinburgh Centenary Series (Oxford: Regnum Books International, 2015), 93.

²⁷ Ibid., 101.

²⁸ Cf. Christopher B. James, "Education that is Missional: Toward a Pedagogy for the Missional Church," in *Social Engagement: The Challenge of the Social in Missiological Education*, The 2013 Proceedings of the Association of Professors of Mission (Kentucky: Frist Fruits Press, 2013), 143 (available at http://place.asburyseminary.edu/cgi/viewcontent.cgi?article=1017&context=firstfruitspapers).

Chapter 10

Church as a Holistic and Inclusive Community: Rethinking Liturgy and Mission

Church as an inclusive community can only be a holistic community. It is with this argument that I begin my essay on the theme, "Church as a holistic community—Liturgy, mission and the inclusive community."

It is also important to chart out the premises of my theological reflections. First, I reflect as a Christian. Second, I am a trained theologian (I hold a doctorate in Systematic Theology). Third, I am a person with disability (PWD).

- Do I need to define church to an august gathering of church leaders? Well, let me try to define what I mean by church. Church is a "called out community" of believers (those who believe) to be a fellowship of those who practice an **alternative lifestyle**. Church cannot be a conformist community. It is a radical fellowship. It is to such a community that Jesus said, "I will build my church."

- In light of what I mentioned above, the mission of the church should also be of an alternative vision—a holistic mission. An inclusive community means the church in its lifestyle has to be inclusive and therefore holistic. So is her mission, an inclusive mission and a holistic mission.

- Now this raises the question of **theology.** I go back to the age-old definition by St. Anselm. Theology is "faith seeking understanding." Theology is the 'outcome' of the interaction(s) of the relationship between God-Human-Creation. Theology in that sense is **doing**. It is practical in its content and nature. Therefore, theology is praxiological. It is such a praxiological theology that we turn our attention to now—disability theology.

Disability Defined (Clarified)

The concept of disability and the idea that 'the disabled' might form a distinct group is historically recent. The genesis of the idea is intricate but there are evidences to show that it developed primarily for administrative reasons, parallel to the establishment of residential institutions for disabled people who were unable to contribute to the industrialised workforce or (perhaps more significantly) were considered to hamper their families' productivity.[1] It was also closely connected to the growing standardisation of the body through advances in medical science, especially to medicine's ability to define standards in quantitative terms.[2]

Until recently, the prevailing framework for understanding disability was provided by the medical model in which disability is a nominative pathology; it is a disease, degeneration, defect or deficit located in an individual. More specifically, it is defined as impairment.

As noted earlier, disability studies is comparatively new to the field of social science. Michael Oliver proposed a social model of disability. It defines disability as the product of specific social and economic structures and aims at addressing issues of oppression and discrimination of disabled people caused by institutional forms of exclusion and by cultural attitudes embedded in social practices.[3] It aptly differentiates between impairment and disability. According to the World Health Organization (WHO), there is a difference between impairment and disability.

Impairment is the abnormality in the structure of the functioning of the body, whether through disease or trauma. Disability is referred to as the restriction in the ability to perform tasks. And handicap is the social disadvantage that could be associated with either impairment and/or disability.[4]

Even though there is an intrinsic relationship between the individual model (individual "abnormality" linked to certain inabilities in performing tasks and, therefore, to disadvantages) and the social model (disability as social construction), the latter is more "disabling" because it is about attitude.

My context is India, and about it we have earlier mentioned in detail. However, a word is in order here. In India with its huge population and rampant poverty the issue of disability hardly finds a mention in the mainstream. However, in recent years we notice a sea of changes that are happening.

It is in such a context that we raise the question of relationship between Church and Disability. PWDs are religiously ostracised too. Deborah Creamer says, "The church has often been unhelpful and even harmful, as it has related to people with disabilities."

She further states, "Historically disabilities have been looked at as a symbol of sin (to be avoided), images of saintliness (to be admired), signs of God's limited power or capriciousness (to be pondered), or suffering personified (to be pitied)—very rarely were people with disabilities considered first as people."[5]

PWDs are not just objects or recipients of the life of the church but also equal partners and subjects of it. That can happen only when the church, in its life, ministry and practices, become inclusive. Recently a friend of mine, while defining an inclusive church, said that an inclusive church is "where liturgy and homiletics are PWD friendly. Where Jesus is not presented only as a healer but also as a nurturer of the lives and faith of his creation." Liturgy is an important aspect of the ministry of the church.

Liturgy and Disability

Liturgy (*leitourgia*) is a Greek composite word meaning a public duty, a service to the state undertaken by a citizen. It can also mean a public performance (in response to the rites performed by the leader) by people.

It is a religious phenomenon, a customary worship/rite performed by a specific religious group according to its traditions. It is a communal response to the sacred through an activity that reflects praise, thanksgiving, supplication or repentance.

Methods of dress, preparation of food, application of cosmetics or other hygienic practices are all considered liturgical activities.

In the Septuagint, it (and the verb *leitourgeo*) is used for the public service of the temple (e.g., Exo. 38:27; 39:12, etc.). Thereafter it comes to have a religious meaning as the function of the priests and the ritual service of the temple (e.g., Joel 1:9, 2:17, etc.). In the New Testament, this religious meaning becomes definitely established. In Luke 1:23, Zechariah goes home when "the days of his liturgy" (*ai hemerai tes leitourgias autou*) are over. In Hebrews 8:6, the High Priest of the New Law "has obtained a better liturgy."

In Christian use, liturgy means the public service(s) of the church. Churches differ on the usage of the word liturgy. Commonly it is distinguished in two senses, namely:

- It is the complex of official services, all the rites, ceremonies, prayers, preaching of the Word and sacraments of the church—as opposed to devotions. It is the rites of the church.

- In the Eastern Churches, liturgy often means the chief official service only—the sacrament of the Holy Eucharist.

Grace comes to us when we receive a sacrament. The minister of the sacrament (usually a priest or deacon) performs the sign of the sacrament and that sign is an action of Christ that brings us grace. For example, in the sacrament of baptism, the priest says, "I baptise you in the name of the Father, and of the Son, and of the Holy Spirit." These words and the act of baptism with water "washes away" the sin of the individual. The individual is in a state of grace. What about PWDs? Are they also included in this sign of grace?

Catholic theologian Edward Foley, who worked among people with intellectual disabilities, writes: "The focus of our reflections was the expressed difficulty that people with intellectual disabilities often experience with sacraments, namely, that many are often refused sacraments because they do not appear to have reached the 'age of reason.' Over the course of our sharing and eventual writing together, I gained many insights about the dynamics of sacramental events that included the participation of people with developmental disabilities. A key insight came from Dianne Bergant, whose reflections on the Hebrew Scriptures helped me understand that 'anomalous' ritual experiences (such as those confronting the chosen people during the period of the exile) **required not only the redefinition of criteria for access, but also a new model for thinking what it means to be human."**[6]

He further mentions his experience:

Communion was an unusual dance with Jamie (a boy with developmental disability in his church) and one that the family had to teach me. It was also one I did not lead. Jamie always came down the aisle walking next to his father, who had instructed me that it was best that he gave Jamie the bread. When they approached, the father took a host from the outstretched paten which I held, and gave his son communion with the traditional text, "Body of Christ." It was only after Jamie had received and consumed that the father turned to me, signalling that he was ready to receive, after which I administered communion to him with the traditional text. It was a small moment in our Eucharistic worship to be sure, probably unnoticed by the vast majority of the other ministers and members of the assembly. Furthermore, it did not occur every week, since I rotated through the presiding schedule on Sunday mornings. On the other hand, in the dozen years that I preached and presided in that community, this Eucharistic dance happened with enough frequency and regularity that it made an indelible impression on me. At the time, I did not have adequate language to frame this unfamiliar dance that disrupted the Eucharistic pattern I had practiced for decades.

> I want to clarify that in that Eucharistic dance with Jamie and his father, I was not the only one with power. Furthermore, it does not appear that the brunt of the human power in that event resided with either me or the father. Instead, it was Jamie—his needs, his moods, his capacities, and his well-being—who was the dictating force in the Eucharistic exchange. This is not to say that all power resided in him, for each one of us in this liturgical triad had the power of engagement, collusion, or resistance."[7]

Liturgical adjustments, redefinitions and reformulations are needed to make disability part and parcel of Christian worship.

Liturgy is celebration of God's grace both in the individual and corporate life of the believers. As such, it includes every lived experience of those who 'participate' in it. That includes PWDs too. The *EDAN-WCC Interim Statement–A Church of All and for All*[8] gives a few practical suggestions towards a liturgical reformulation of the church in the light of the lived experiences of PWDs. I have quoted a few of them here:

73. God's reign is a present reality. Everyone including the ignored, forgotten, left out, and people with physical and mental impairments and chronic illness are invited to the feast. How does it affect our worship if, instead of inviting only those whose patterns of behaviour, speech and preferences are known, we extent an open invitation to all?

74. Common worship is the most evident expression of a community. For the liturgy to be truly the work of the people and to accommodate the participation of all the gathered body in worship, we may need to reconfigure our space, reimagine how we do liturgy and reconsider the role each person plays. Both the drama of liturgy and the drama of disability deal with the fragility of our lives and our dependence upon God. We need to be able to bring our struggles into our worship so that the

symbols of the liturgy will be meaningful to us. Symbolically, this is God's banquet table. The question is: have we made it possible for everyone who so desires to get there, to partake of the feast and to join the conversation? In this gathered body, will there be a place for each person? To ensure that all can participate in worship means we need to consider how our experience and expression of liturgy engages the whole person; physical movement, senses and intellect. People with learning difficulties respond to the integrity of a congregation. They pick up the real and true involvement of those around them and respond to that devotion.

75. Great significance has been ascribed to words in our teaching and worship, particularly in the Protestant traditions. The "word" of God is an important and vital part of our faith. Bible passages introduce us to people and events, recount the history of God's relationship to humankind, teach us about God's ways and guide our lives today. The words of sermons, prayers and hymns can stimulate our minds and reach into the depths of our hearts to provoke, inspire or console us. The words we use have the power to create images and define our identities and relationships. Too often, they have not sounded tidings of good news or portrayed messages of hope to people with disabilities. Indeed, too often, children and persons with learning difficulties can be excluded from full participation "because they do not understand." They, along with people who are poor, homeless, sick, in prison or struggling with addictions, are often referred to in the third person as "those" in the prayers and texts our churches frequently use. This makes it sound as if these people are not an integral part of the congregation. We need to monitor our patterns of speech that create binaries of an "us/them" relationship that casts the disabled person as the outsider, the other.

76. Metaphors can also alienate some of our brothers and sisters. Equating a lack of compassion, an unwillingness to listen, or a lack of resolve to being blind, mentally ill, deaf or paralysed is disparaging and disempowering. By articulating our strengths or identity in terms that disparage persons who live with such physical or mental impairments, we align ourselves against them; we shut them out. Perhaps unintentionally, we project on them what is fearful or negative in ourselves and cast them as the embodiment of evil. The phrase "we are disfigured by sin" from a prayer of confession is an example of this insensitivity. It is doubtful that these words would bring solace to any person living with burn scars or facial deformity. Ways to express these passages and metaphors in an inclusive manner in our sermons, liturgies and hymns be found. *Language has power ("Death and life are in the power of the tongue …." Pro. 18:21) to suppress others. How true it is of PWDs when they are "named" or categorised by languages that are extremely hurtful.*

77. All these words and expressions can stimulate thinking and help clarify certain points. But to follow such discourse can be tiresome or confusing for people with little education, short attention spans, cognitive disabilities or other mental impairments. Sometimes people "hear" or comprehend God's word, and know the mystery and majesty of God's presence in their lives through a sensory experience: perception of light or colour, a picture or sculpture, a whiff of incense, silence, music, dance, a procession, a hug or clasped hands around a circle. This sensory experience in liturgy is important to all of us, but especially to children, elderly people and persons with disabilities. It should be considered in our planning of corporate worship and its setting. *Liturgy as experience/experience as liturgy. The church has to find ways to include the lived experiences of PWDs in the liturgical life of the church too to make it inclusive.*

78. Many elements of worship are non-verbal, and we can be more intentional about how we incorporate them to enhance the service for everyone. There is the movement of dance, drama, hands clasped in prayer or raised in blessing, making the sign of the cross, handshakes and hugs, lifting the eyes, bowing the head, offering gifts, and passing the bread and cup. There are tactile elements of anointing, baptism, laying-on of hands, foot-washing, touching and vesting. We can smell the incense, wine, flowers, and candles and taste the bread and wine or juice. Besides words, we hear music, clapping, bells, sighs and breathing. Centuries ago when many did not know how to read or have access to printed material, churches were filled with visual renditions of the Bible stories. There were murals, tapestries, sculpture, icons and stained-glass windows. Today, some churches still have many of these visual elements and can also make use of banners, altar hangings, colourful vestments, scarves, flowers, balloons, liturgical dance and drama to portray the messages of our faith. *Non-verbal modes of liturgical expressions too be included in the worship services to make it more inclusive both in content and practice.*

79. For people who do not hear well, there should be much to see; for those with very little vision, there should be much to hear. Verbal cues from the minister or liturgist are helpful to a person who is blind. Otherwise s/he may spend all the service trying to figure out when s/he should be sitting or kneeling or standing. All that needs to be said is, "You may rise" or "You may be seated." For individuals who have difficulty sitting still for very long, there should be opportunities to move. There should always be a place for some to sit even if everyone else is standing for part or all of the service. At a service where the people are seated on the floor or ground, some sort of chair

or bench should be provided for people who cannot safely get down or up from such a position. Some people cannot kneel or climb steps safely, so communion needs to be brought to their level. A clear path of travel and sure footing with no stairs is necessary for those unsteady on their feet. In the arrangement of space, people who use wheelchairs need to have seating choices so that they can sit with family and friends as part of the gathered body; they should not be limited to a space way in front or far behind everyone else or stuck out in an aisle. Several pews can be shortened to make space for wheelchairs.

80. Acoustics will be particularly important for people who are blind or hard of hearing. Individuals with limited sight rely more on their hearing, and those who are hard of hearing need good public-address systems to amplify the voice of the preacher or liturgist. Individual assistive listening devices (ALDs) that can be used with and without hearing aids may be particularly useful. Good lighting is crucial for persons with limited vision so they can make optimum use of the sight they do have. It is important for people who are deaf or hard of hearing that they can see the speaker's lips or the sign-language interpreter. A printed order of worship may be particularly helpful to people with hearing impairments. Copies can easily be produced in large print (size 18 font on a computer or enlarged on a photocopier) for people with limited vision. Large-print Bibles are available and music for a service can be enlarged on a photocopier. Overhead projectors and computers can also be used to display print material in a large format for a whole congregation. While only a small percentage of people who are blind know how to read Braille, for those who do, this may be an important way to make the liturgy more accessible. Braille books, including Bibles and hymnals, take up a lot of space, so

some congregations keep the pages in loose-leaf binders and remove only the ones needed for a particular service. When the service is over, the pages are put back for use another time.

81. Besides the physical accommodations such as lighting, sound systems and appropriate seating that can make a space accessible to everyone, we need to consider the attitudes and behaviour patterns that can create barriers for people with disabilities or cause some to feel unwelcome or left out. To feel truly welcome in the church, persons with disabilities need to see people like themselves in leadership roles. For people with disabilities to play a larger role, a faith community may need to rethink its policies about who is and who is not allowed to offer welcome, usher, or participate as banner-bearer, to sing in the choir, to read the lessons and lead the prayers of the people. Is the altar area accessible to someone who uses a wheelchair or walker? Can the microphone be adjusted to different heights? Inclusion requires the conviction of the disabled person that he/she has access to leadership according to his/her abilities, attitudes and vocations, setting aside his/her complexes and frustrations.

82. Rigid codes of "acceptable" behaviour may need to be loosened. Just as some people cannot stand or kneel, others cannot sit still for a whole hour or more. They may need to stand or move about because of back pain or muscle spasms or some agitation related to their disability. Some may not be able to understand the "rules" about silence and may mumble to themselves, speak out when others are quietly listening or utter exuberant vocalisations at unexpected moments. In these situations, as with people who "make a joyful noise unto the Lord" by singing off-key, we can acquire tolerance that

acknowledges such behaviour as a mild distraction rather than a great annoyance.

As noted earlier, liturgy is the outward expression of the worship and many a times these expressions have not been inclusive both in its content and practice. As a PWD, I can say it with confidence that at least in my "churchly" life, liturgical expressions have not been inclusive. It does not need a huge amount of change to become inclusive. It just needs a change of attitude and perspective. Is the church ready to embrace this change?

Discussions from a disability perspective about church, mission, holisticity, inclusivity and liturgy would radically reshape our theological conversations and practical theology. I conclude here by reminding ourselves that "Only an inclusive church is a holistic church."

Endnotes

[1] C. Barnes, G. Mercer, and T. Shakespeare, *Exploring Disability: a Sociological Introduction* (Cambridge: Polity Press, 1999), 18-20.

[2] J. Leach Scully, "A Postmodern Disorder: Moral Encounters with Molecular Models of Disability," in *Disability/Postmodernity: Embodying Disability Theory*, ed. M. Corker and T. Shakespeare (London: Continuum, 2002), 48-61. Quoted in Jackie Leach Scully, "Drawing Lines, Crossing Lines: Ethics and the Challenge of Disabled Embodiment," *Feminist Theology: The Journal of the Britain & Ireland School of Feminist Theology* 11, no. 3 (2003): 266.

[3] Lorella Terzi, "The Social Model of Disability: A Philosophical Critique," *Journal of Applied Philosophy* 21, no. 2 (2004): 141.

[4] Quoted in ibid., 142.

[5] Deborah Creamer, "Theological Accessibility: The Contribution of Disability," *Disability Studies Quarterly* 26, no. 4 (Fall 2006). http://www.dsq-sds.org/article/view/812/987 (accessed September 29, 2010).

[6] Edward Foley, "Eucharist, Postcolonial Theory and Developmental Disabilities: A Practical Theologian Revisits the Jesus Table," *International Journal of Practical Theology* 15, no. 1 (2011): 70 (57-73).

[7] Ibid.

[8] "A Church of All and for All: An Interim Statement", http://www.oikoumene.org/en/resources/documents/wcc-commissions/faith-and-order-commission/ix-other-study-processess/a-church-of-all-and-for-all-an-interim-statement?set_language=en (accessed 2 December 2013).

Church as "Eyes" and "Feet" to PWDs
Job 29:15

Chapter 29 contains reminiscences of Job's previous blessed condition. A condition where he had good health and wealth. However, now he has neither. He argues with God that he does not deserve the present "disabling" situation. In his defence (to God and his friends), Job lists the benefits he brought to those in need. He "was eyes to the blind," indicating that he would guide them to their destination. He was "feet to the lame" by carrying them or having them carried by his servants. For Job, the blessed condition was when he was "eyes" and "feet" to persons with disabilities (PWDs).

There is a lesson for the church in this passage. The church is called to be a catalyst to spur PWDs to life in its fullness. In its life, ministry and mission, the church is called to be the "eyes" and "feet" with and to PWDs. This can happen only when the church identifies with PWDs, not as objects, but as subjects. The church's identification with PWDs is a reversal of role.

The "condition of blessedness" that Job speaks in the passage is a "condition of inclusion." It is in including OTHERS or BECOMING OTHERS that Job experiences blessedness. The blessedness of the church is dependent on its inclusion of OTHERS. "Blessed are the poor in spirit, for theirs is the kingdom of heaven." (Matt. 5:3) Job made the choice by including OTHERS in his life.

How can the church both experience blessedness and be an agent of radical inclusivity? This passage shows that it is possible to experience and practice both—by including OTHERS (here PWDs) in the life, ministry and mission of the church.

Who Sinned?
John 9:1-41

This text represents one of the clearest incidents of Jesus healing a person with disability. Jesus heals a person with visual impairment, one who had been blind from birth. Interestingly, the whole chapter is about the interplay of sin and disability. Disability then and now is seen as the tangible manifestation of sin.

The disciples of Jesus did not see the person but the disability he had. It is something that PWDs often face. Their identity is from their disability. The person behind the disability is conveniently neglected or rejected. And the next thing they see is who is responsible for his disability. They have been brought up in a religio-cultural context where disability is associated with generational sin. Therefore, the question, "Who sinned?"

Jesus confronts the settled notion prevalent among Jews, here exhibited by the disciples' question, "Rabbi, who sinned, this man or his parents, that he was born blind?" (v.2). He rejects it categorically and says, "Neither this man nor his parents sinned; he was born blind so that God's works might be revealed in him" (v.4).

From a disability perspective, Jesus said only that the life of the man born blind would be lived for the glory of God, not that God somehow was the cause of the man's blindness. Nor does he approve his disciples' position that sin begets disability.

The passage demands an answer from Jesus. However, Jesus does not let him be dragged into the answers they have. He shatters their notion of sin.

In the context of the story, sin here is committed by others (symbolised by the disciples, the neighbours, the crowd, the Pharisees, the temple authorities). Jesus turns the table on them and confronts them: "It is you who have sinned against this man. All of you did not see the person in him but his disability." Disability, as we have noted earlier in this volume, is imposed by society on PWDs. Here too, in this passage, Jesus offers a counter-narrative that it is society that sins against persons with disabilities.

Afterword

*M.C. Thomas**

Since I was asked to write a reflection on the church and disability, let me begin with a personal note. I am an ordained clergy of the Mar Thoma Church with 35 years of pastoral ministry. I continue to be in the teaching ministry in biblical studies at the Mar Thoma Theological Seminary, Kottayam, Kerala, under the Senate of Serampore College in India. I was diagnosed with Multiple Sclerosis (MS) in 2007 and have been undergoing treatment. The nature of MS manifested in different ways, and my physical condition gradually declined and finally it brought me to a wheelchair in 2015. Now I know what it means to be disabled physically, having lost movement in the lower limb of my body, which has helped me understand the vulnerability and the value of the life that God has given us. In this regard, the following theological reflections on church and disability will be grounded on my personal experience based on my physical infirmity.

Disability as a Window to New Horizons

I understand that disability functions as a window to new horizons of visions, both to the church and to the disabled. It genuinely challenges the public and popular understanding of one's phenomenological being-ness because media commercials present a perfect and healthy person as a "Complete Man." It has its own biases, based on class, caste, gender, religion, etc., through which the dominant society exercises its authority and power. A society that functions on the basis of such parameters has a different perception of life in which disability is considered unfortunate, a curse. Some kind of otherness has inherently been inscribed on disability, which eventually leads to alienation and marginalisation.

The church is set in this popular phenomenological context as the body of Christ. The very identity of the church as a corporate body must be rearticulated contrary to the process through which the dominant society designs its world; it is to be renegotiated and reconstructed in the discourses of the church. The worldview and the planning of the dominant society are not with an inclusive vision that recognises the presence and the need of the differently-abled in society. For instance, as a person living in India, when I look at the overall planning and architectural structure of an Indian township, including places of worship, the needs of the physically challenged are ignored. It is quite evident in the lack of parking space for the physically challenged, the nonexistence of a ramp and an elevator, the absence of wheelchair pathways and wheelchair-friendly doors for public transportation and so on. All this reveal the worldview and perceptions of life maintained by that society. Here, the church must envision its identity as the body of Christ where all are equally important and all are welcome. We believe that humans are created in the image of God and that image must be recognised in all bodies, including disembodied bodies. With this different vision, the church needs to engage with society so that the doors are opened to extend hospitality to the disabled "other" in society.

On the other side, disability functions as a window to the disabled as they confront different sets of psychological, mental, spiritual and physical problems. To lead a life with a difference seems to be quite difficult for the disabled. When disability is confronted as a challenge to face the God-given life differently, it appears to be a window to multiple possibilities through which one can reconfigure life to step into one's consequent responsibilities with a different theological vision of life.

Furthermore, disability is seen as a window for the church through which it envisions its mission and ministry differently. In this process, as Emmanuel Levinas suggests, the church must see the face of the other differently, as the living presence of others experienced ethically and socially. In this process of seeing the face of the other, the church experiences its being along with its welcoming of the disabled unreservedly with an alternative vision. In this radical vision, we acknowledge and affirm that God has a preferential option for the disabled as the vulnerable who are privileged in the sight of God. They are not the least and the lost ones of society; rather they are the privileged ones who received special care from the "Good Shepherd" as narrated in the parable of the lost sheep (Lk. 15). Moreover, just as we read in 2 Cor. 12:9, the power of God is manifested in the weakness of the vulnerable through the abundant grace of God, where vulnerability can function as a tool for the transformation and liberation of God's creation in its totality.

Sickness and disability was approached and appreciated differently by ancient Judaean society, which has been represented both in the Old and the New Testaments. Sickness was generally considered either a curse or a judgment by God for sin and rebellion. It is reflected in the healing narrative of the paralytic in Mark 2: 1-12; Jesus healed the paralytic by pronouncing "Son, your sins are forgiven" (v.5). Moreover, the disembodied ones did not have a place in ritual practices; religious space and practices were intended to be officiated by "perfected bodies," which must be predominantly the bodies of men. The interpretation of the law and the legal practices developed, mainly, during the post-exilic period which sanctioned the legitimacy of such practices in ancient Judaism where the otherness of the disabled was not positively appreciated and accepted.

But the Bible apparently provides a different theological vision of an embodied life which has its grounding in the creation stories in Gen. 1-3; we read about the sabbath as the celebration of the wholeness in the divinely created order which must obviously be realised and envisioned through inclusivity and hospitality. There has always been a place and acceptance of the so-called 'other' in an inclusive community. But unfortunately, such 'otherness' has been defined differently based on multiple parameters determined by the dominant structures of power of the corresponding societies. Contrary to such parameters of the dominant society, the Bible provides an alternative vision of healing, embodiment and inclusivity which has been imagined as the realisation of the shalom experience in the New Heaven and New Earth (Isa. 65: 17-25; Rev. 21). Such an alternative imagination was exercised and executed by Jesus in his healing ministry of the kingdom of God.

***The Rev. Dr. M.C. Thomas** serves the Mar Thoma Theological Seminary and the Federated Faculty for Research in Religion and Culture (FFRRC), Kottayam, as Professor of Old Testament.

Bibliography

Books, Book Sections, Journal/Magazine Articles:

Barnes, C., G. Mercer, and T. Shakespeare. *Exploring Disability: A Sociological Introduction*. Cambridge: Polity Press, 1999.

Bevans, Stephen. "Theological Education as Missionary Formation." In *Reflecting on and Equipping for Christian Mission*, edited by Stephen Bevans et al., Regnum Edinburgh Centenary Series, 93-105. Oxford: Regnum Books International, 2015.

Block, Jennie Weiss. *Copious Hosting: A Theology of Access for People with Disabilities*. New York: Continuum International Publishing Group Ltd., 2002.

Bosch, David J. *Transforming Mission: Paradigm Shifts in Theology of Mission*. Maryknoll, New York: Orbis Books, 1991.

Botha, Nico, K.K. Kritzinger, and Tinyiko Maluleke, "Crucial issues for Christian Mission – A Missiological Analysis of Contemporary South Africa." *International Review of Mission* 83, no. 328 (January, 1986): 21-36.

Boulton, Wayne G., Thomas D. Kennedy, and Alan Verhey, *From Christ to the World: Introductory Readings in Christian Ethics*. Grand Rapids, Michigan: William B. Eerdmans Publishing Company, 1994.

Castro, Emilio. *Freedom in Mission: The Perspective of the Kingdom of God. An Ecumenical Inquiry*. Geneva: WCC Publications, 1985.

Coleridge, P. *Disability, Liberation and Development*. Oxford: Oxfam, 1993.

Comblin, José. *Retrieving the Human: A Christian Anthropology*. Maryknoll, New York: Orbis Books, 1990.

Cooper, Burton Z. "The Disabled God." *Theology Today* 49, no. 2 (July 1992): 173-82.

Corker, M. "Differences, Conflations and Foundations: The Limits to "Accurate" Theoretical Representation of Disabled People's Experience?" *Disability & Society* 14, no. 5 (1999): 627-42;

Crow, L. "Including All of Our Lives: Renewing the Social Model of Disability." In *Exploring the Divide: Illness and Disability*, edited by C. Barnes and G. Mercer. 55-73. Leeds: The Disability Press, 1996.

Dados, Nour and Raewyn Connell, "The Global South." *Context* 11, no. 1 (Winter 2012): 12-13.

Daggers, Jenny, and Grace Ji-Sun Kim, eds., *Christian Doctrines for Global Gender Justice*. New York: Palgrave Macmillan, 2015.

Desai, Arvindrai N. *Helping the Handicapped: Problems and Prospects*. New Delhi: Ashish Publishing House, 1990.

Ehrman, Terrence. "Disability and Resurrection Identity." *New Blackfriars* 96, no. 1066 (November 2015): 723-738.

Eiesland, Nancy L. *The Disabled God. Towards a Liberatory Theology of Disability*. Nashville: Abingdon Press, 1994.

Erb, Susan, and Barbara Harriss-White. *Outcast from Social Welfare. Adult Disability, Incapacity and Development in Rural South India*. Bangalore: Books for Change, 2002.

Ferdinando, Keith. "Jesus, the Theological Educator," *Themelios* 38, no. 3 (2013): 360-74.

Foley, Edward. "Eucharist, Postcolonial Theory and Developmental Disabilities: A Practical Theologian Revisits the Jesus Table" *International Journal of Practical Theology* 15, no. 1 (2011): 57-73.

Fritzson, Arne, and Samuel Kabue. *Interpreting Disability*. Risk Book. Geneva: WCC Publications, 2004.

George, Samuel. "Persons with Disabilities in India." In *Persons with Disabilities in Society: Problems and Challenges*, edited by Wati Longchar and Gordon Cowans. Vol. I. 33-46. Manila, The Philippines: ATESEA, 2007.

__________. "Voices and Visions from the Margins on Mission and Unity: A Disability-Informed Reading of the Pauline Metaphor of the Church as the Body of Christ." *International Review of Mission* 100, no. 1 (April 2011): 96-103.

__________. "Among the People: A Search for People's Theology." In *Among the People: Essays in Honour of Rev. Dr. P. G. Vargis*, edited by V. D. John and Viju Wilson, 184-193. Delhi: ISPCK & SALT DC, 2012.

__________. "God of Life, Justice and Peace: A Disability Informed Reading of Christology." *The Ecumenical Review* 64, no. 4 (December 2012): 454-63.

__________. "Image of God and Disability, Stigma and Discrimination." In *Sprouts of Disability Theology*, edited by Christopher Rajkumar, 60-65. Nagpur, India: NCCI, 2012.

__________. "Disabilit(Y) Ethics: A Search for a 'Different' Paradigm in Christian Ethics." *Bangalore Theological Forum* XLVIII, no. 1 (June 2016): 74-91.

__________. "Introduction." In *Christian Theology: Indian Conversations*, edited by Samuel George and P. Mohan Larbeer, vii-xvii. Bangalore: BTESSC, 2016.

__________. "Resurrected (yet) Disabled Christ: Resurrected Body and Disability." In *Disability Theology from Asia: A Resource Book for Theological and Religious Studies*, edited by Anjeline Okola and Wati Longchar, 313-322. Kenya/Taiwan/Myanmar/India: EDAN-WCC/PTCA/ATEM/SATHRI/YTCS, 2019.

__________. "Theological Education as Missional Formation: Contributions of the World Council of Churches' Ecumenical Disability Advocates Network." *International Review of Mission* 108, no. 1 (June 2019): 8-17.

Ghai, Anita. "Introduction: Epistemological and Academic Concerns of Disability in the Global South." In *Disability in South Asia: Knowledge and Experience*, edited by Anita Ghai, 23-69. New Delhi: Sage Publications, 2018.

Gill, Robin. *A Textbook of Christian Ethics*. Edinburgh: T. & T. Clark Ltd., 1985.

Haight, Roger. *Dynamics of Theology*. Bangalore: Claretian Publications, 2002.

Hittenberger, Jeff, and Martin William Mittelstadt, "Power and Powerlessness in Pentecostal Theology. A Review Essay on Amos Yong's Theology and Down Syndrome: Reimagining Disability in Late Modernity." *Pneuma* 30 (2008): 137-145.

Hoekendijk, J. C. "The Church in Missionary Thinking." *International Review of Mission* XLI, no. 163 (1952): 324-36.

Jha, Jainendra Kuman, ed., *Encyclopaedia of Social Work*. Lucknow: Institute for Sustainable Development, 2001.

Johnson, Andrew "Turning the World Upside Down in 1 Corinthians 15: Apocalyptic Epistemology, the Resurrected Body and the New Creation." *The Evangelical Quarterly* 75, no. 4 (2004): 291-309.

Katsuno Lynda, and Arne Fritzson, "Disability." In *Dictionary of the Ecumenical Movement*, edited by Nicholas Lossky et al. (Geneva: WCC Publications, 2002), 326-27.

Kritzinger, J. J. *The South African Context for Mission*. Cape Town: Lux Verbi 1988.

Lehmann, Paul L. *Ethics in a Christian Context*. New York: Harper & Row, Publishers, 1976.

Longchar, A. Wati. "Culture, Sin, Suffering and Disability in Society." In *Embracing the Inclusive Community: A Disability Perspective*, edited by A. Wati Longchar and R. Christopher Rajkumar, 65-81. Bangalore: BTESSC/SATHRI, NCCI & SCEPTRE, 2010.

Macquarrie, John. *Principles of Christian Theology*. 2nd ed. New York: Charles Scribner's Sons, 1977.

McCloughry, Roy, and Wayne Morris. *Making a World of Difference: Christian Reflections on Disability*. London: SPCK, 2002.

McGrath, Alister E. *Christian Theology: An Introduction*, 3 ed. Oxford, U.K. & Malden, U.S.A.: Blackwell Publishing Ltd., 2003 [2001].

Mehrotra, Nilika. "Disability Rights Movement in India: Politics and Practice." *Economic and Political Weekly* 46, no. 6 (2011): 65–72.

Migliore, Daniel L. *Faith Seeking Understanding: An Introduction to Christian Theology*. 2nd ed. Michigan, Grand Rapids: William B. Eerdmans Publishing Company, 2004 (1993).

Morris, Jenny. "Impairment and Disability: Constructing an Ethics of Care That Promotes Human Rights." *Hypatia* 16, no. 4 (2001): 1-16.

Moss, Candida R. "Heavenly Healing: Eschatological Cleansing and the Resurrection of the Dead in the Early Church." *Journal of the American Academy of Religion* 79, no. 4 (December 2011): 991-1017.

Murickan, Jose, and Georgekutty Kareparampil. *Persons with Disabilities in Society*. Trivandrum, India: Kerala Federation of the Blind, 1995.

Nelson, J. Robert. "Challenging 'Disabled Theology.'" *Christian Century* 98, no. 39 (December 1981): 1244-45.

Newbigin, Lesslie. "Mission and Missions." *Christianity Today* 4, no. 22 (August 1, 1960): 911.

Newell, Christopher. "Disability, Bioethics, and Rejected Knowledge." *Journal of Medicine & Philosophy* 31, no. 3 (2006): 269-83.

Oliver, M. *The Politics of Disablement*. Basingstoke: Macmillan, 1990.

__________. *Understanding Disability: From Theory to Practice*. Basingstoke: Palgrave, 1996.

Panikkar, Raimundo. *The Trinity and the Religious Experience of Man, Icon-Person-Mystery*. London: Darton, Longman and Todd, 1979.

Panneberg, Wolfhart. *Systematic Theology*, vol. 2. Grand Rapids, Michigan & Edinburgh: William B. Eerdmans Publishing Company & T & T Clark Ltd., 1994.

Pillay, Jerry. "Theological Foundation of Mission." In *Mission Continues: Global Impulses for the 21st Century*, edited by Claudia Währisch-Oblau and Fidon Mwombeki, Regnum Edinburgh 2010 Series, 7-17. Oxford: Regnum Books International, 2010.

Polkinghorne, John. "Eschatology Credibility: Emergent and Teleological Processes." In *Resurrection: Theological and Scientific Assessments*, edited by Ted Peters, Robert J. Russell and Michael Welker, 43-55. Grand Rapids, Michigan: William B. Eerdmans Publishing Company, 2002.

Rahner, Karl. *Meditations on the Sacraments*. New York: Seabury Press, 1977.

Raphael, Rebecca. "Things Too Wonderful: A Disabled Reading of Job." *Perspectives in Religious Studies* 31, no. 4 (Winter 2004): 399-424.

Reinders, Hans S. *Receiving the Gift of Friendship: Profound Disability, Theological Anthropology, and Ethics*. Grand Rapids, Michigan & Cambridge, U.K.: William B. Eerdmans Publishing Company, 2008.

Reynolds, Thomas E. *Vulnerable Communion: A Theology of Disability and Hospitality*. Michigan: Brazos Press, 2008.

Scully, Jackie Leach. "A Postmodern Disorder: Moral Encounters with Molecular Models of Disability." In *Disability/Postmodernity: Embodying Disability Theory*, edited by M. Corker and T. Shakespeare. 48-61. London: Continuum, 2002.

__________. "Drawing Lines, Crossing Lines: Ethics and the Challenge of Disabled Embodiment." *Feminist Theology: The Journal of the Britain & Ireland School of Feminist Theology* 11, no. 3 (2003): 265-80.

Senior, Donald "Beware of the Canaanite Woman: Disability and the Bible." In *Religion and Disability: Essays in Scripture, Theology and Ethics*, edited by Marylin E. Bishop, 1-26. Kansas City: Sheed & Ward, 1995.

Sunny, Shashi. "Sounds of Silence." *People* April 6, 2012, 104-106.

Swinton, John. *Resurrecting the Person: Friendship and the Care of People with Mental Health Problems*. Nashville: Abingdon Press, 2000.

—————. "The Body of Christ Has Down's Syndrome: Theological Reflections on Vulnerability, Disability, and Graceful Communities." *Journal of Pastoral Theology* 13, no. 2 (September 2003): 66-78.

—————. *Dementia: Living in the Memories of God*. Grand Rapids, Michigan: William B. Eerdmans Publishing Company, 2012.

Terzi, Lorella. "The Social Model of Disability: A Philosophical Critique." *Journal of Applied Philosophy* 21, no. 2 (2004): 141-57.

Thompson, Luke S. Carlos A. "Moving Beyond the Limits of Disability Inclusion: Using the Concept of Belonging Through Friendship to Improve the Outcome of the Social Model of Disability." *International Journal of Humanities and Social Sciences* 10, no. 5 (2016): 1488-91.

Verkuyl, J. *Contemporary Missiology: An Introduction*. Grand Rapids, Michigan: William B. Eerdmans Publishing Company, 1978.

WHO's report on disability (2011).

Wilfred, Felix. *Margins: Site of Asian Theologies*. Delhi: ISPCK, 2008.

Wilhelm, Dorothée. "Women with Disabilities A Challenge to Feminist Theology. Roundtable Discussion." *Journal of Feminist Studies in Religion* 10, no. 2 (Fall 1994): 104-08.

Wynn, Kerry H. "The Normate Hermeneutic and Interpretation of Disability within the Yahwistic Narratives." In *This Abled Body: Rethinking Disabilities in Biblical Studies*, edited by Hector Avalos, Sarah J. Melcher, and Jeremy Schipper, 91-101. Atlanta: Society of Biblical Literature, 2007.

Young, Amos. "Disability and the Gifts of the Spirit: Pentecost and the Renewal of the Church." *Journal of Pentecostal Theology* 19, no. 1 (2010): 86-89.

—————. "Disability and the Gifts of the Spirit: Pentecost and the renewal of the church." *Journal of Pentecostal Theology* 19, no. 1 (2010), 76-93.

Zutshi, Bupinder. *Disability Status in India- Case Study of Delhi Metropolitan Region*. New Delhi: PhD Centre for the Study of Regional Development, Jawaharlal Nehru University, September 2004.

Websites

http://www.disabilityindia.org. Accessed on 01/04/2007.

Creamer, Deborah. "Theological Accessibility: The Contribution of Disability." *Disability Studies* Quarterly 26, no. 4 (Fall 2006). http://www.dsq-sds. org/article/view/812/987 (accessed September 29, 2010).

"A Church of All and for All: An Interim Statement." http://www.oikoumene. org/en/resources/documents/wcc-commissions/faith-and-order-commission/ix-other-study-processess/a-church-of-all-and-for-all-an-interim-statement?set_language=en (accessed December 02, 2013).

http://www.tamu.edu/faculty/choudhury/culture.html (accessed October 24, 2012).

http://www.oikoumene.org/en/news/news-management/eng/a/article/3591/2013-assembly-theme-g.html (accessed September 01, 2012).

Sridhar, Lalitha. "70 million disabled in India, and only 2% are educated and 1% employed," *Infochange* (September 30, 2010). http://infochangeindia. org/2003060269/Disabilities/Features/70-million-disabled-in-India-and-only-2-are-educated-and-1-employed.html (accessed September 30, 2010).

India Office of the Registrar General & Census Commissioner, http:// censusindia.gov.in/Census_And_You/disabled_population.aspx (accessed September 30, 2010).

http://www.raimon-panikkar.org/english/gloss-cosmotheandric.html (accessed October 09, 2016).

Pilario, Daniel Franklin. "Doing Theology from the Margins: Experience and Reflections." http://www.svst.edu.ph/doing-theology-from-the-margins.html (accessed October 05, 2016).

https://www.oikoumene.org/en/resources/documents/wcc-programmes/justice-diakonia-and-responsibility-for-creation/diakonia (accessed June 17, 2020).

https://stpaulcarlisle.org/diaconal-ministry/ (accessed June 17, 2020).

http://www.edan-wcc.org/index.php/about-us/history (accessed January 08, 2016).

http://www.edan-wcc.org/index.php/about-us/who-we-are (accessed January 08, 2016).

James, Christopher B. "Education that is Missional: Toward a Pedagogy for the Missional Church." In *Social Engagement: The Challenge of the Social in Missiological Education*, *The 2013 Proceedings of the Association of Professors of Mission*. Kentucky: Frist Fruits Press, 2013, 141-164. (available at http://place.asburyseminary.edu/cgi/viewcontent.cgi?article=1017&context=firstfruitspapers)

https://www.youtube.com/watch?v=hOCQJt92ScE&feature=youtu.be (accessed November 06, 2018)

Nancy Eiesland, "Encountering the Disabled God," The Other Side (September & October 2002), 12-13. http://www.dsfnetwork.org/assets/Uploads/DisabilitySunday/21206.Eiesland-Disabled-God.pdf (accessed November 10, 2018).

Chong, Shiao. "The Disabled Savior." *The Banner* (March 3, 2017), https://www.thebanner.org/features/2017/03/the-disabled-savior (accessed November 10, 2018).

www.ingramcontent.com/pod-product-compliance
Lightning Source LLC
Chambersburg PA
CBHW022007120726
47992CB00001B/453